by
Barbara Getty & Inga Dubay

Handwriting Success™
Portland, Oregon USA

GETTY-DUBAY™ ITALIC HANDWRITING SERIES

BOOK A ▪ Basic Italic
14 mm body height

BOOK B ▪ Basic Italic
11 mm, 9 mm body height

BOOK C ▪ Basic & Cursive Italic
9 mm, 6 mm body height   Introduction to Cursive Italic

BOOK D ▪ Basic & Cursive Italic
6 mm, 5 mm body height

BOOK E ▪ Basic & Cursive Italic
6 mm, 5 mm, 4 mm body height

BOOK F ▪ Basic & Cursive Italic
6 mm, 5 mm, 4 mm body height

BOOK G ▪ Basic & Cursive Italic
5 mm, 4 mm body height

INSTRUCTION MANUAL

INTERNATIONAL EDITION
Copyright 2011, 2013 by Barbara M. Getty and Inga S. Dubay
ISBN 978-1-7334352-0-8

FOURTH EDITION
Copyright 2011, 2013 by Barbara M. Getty and Inga S. Dubay
THIRD EDITION
Copyright 1994 by Barbara M. Getty and Inga S. Dubay
SECOND EDITION
Copyright 1986 by Barbara M. Getty and Inga S. Dubay
REVISED EDITION
Copyright 1980 by Barbara M. Getty and Inga S. Dubay
FIRST EDITION
Copyright 1979 by Barbara M. Getty and Inga S. Dubay

All rights reserved.
This text may not be reproduced in whole or in part
without the express written permission of the copyright holder.

Handwriting Success, LLC
Portland, Oregon USA
www.handwritingsuccess.com

Printed at various locations around the world via IngramSpark.

Cover Design: Sinda Markham
Front cover picture: Cedar Creek near Cottage Grove, Oregon USA
Back cover pictures: Newt crawling over lichen on the forest floor, Indian-pipe flowers

CONTENTS

iv	Basic & Cursive Italic Alphabet
v	Introduction
vi	Reminders
viii	Assessment Pre-test/Post-test
1	**PART ONE:** *Getty-Dubay™ Basic Italic*
2	Lowercase Families 1–4
3	Lowercase Families 5–8 (9 mm height)
4	Lowercase Families 1–6
5	Lowercase Families 7–8 (5 mm height)
6	Capital Families
7	Capital Letters: large, small, mixed
8	Numerals
10	Writing Practice
13	Handwriting Tips
15	**PART TWO:** *Getty-Dubay™ Cursive Italic*
16	Capitals A B C D E F G H
17	Capitals I J K L M N O P Q
18	Capitals R S T U V W X Y Z
19	Transition to Cursive Lowercase
20	Review
21	Join 1
22	Join 2
24	Join 3
25	Join 4
26	Join 5
28	Join 6
29	Join 7
30	Join 8
31	Lifts
32	Writing Practice
38	Timed Writing
39	Options
40	Slope and Spacing Guidelines
41	**PART THREE:** *Getty-Dubay™ Edged Pen Italic*
42	Italic with Edged Pen
43	Basic Italic
45	Cursive Italic & Joins 1–2
47	Joins 3–8
49	Cursive Capitals
51	Chancery Cursive
53	Pangrams (alphabet sentences)
56	Personal Correspondence
57	Greeting Card & Surprise Booklet
58	Glossary
59	Bibliography
60	5° Letter Slope Lines
61	5 mm Lines
62	4 mm Lines

Getty-Dubay™ ITALIC HANDWRITING SERIES
BASIC & CURSIVE ITALIC ALPHABET

BASIC ITALIC

*All letters written in one stroke unless otherwise indicated. All letters start at the top except lowercase **d** and **e**.*

Aa Bb Cc Dd Ee Ff Gg
or A   or e

Hh Ii Jj Kk Ll Mm
or h   or M

Nn Oo Pp Qq Rr Ss Tt
or n   or t

Uu Vv Ww Xx Yy Zz

0 1 2 3 4 5 6 7 8 9
     or 4   or 7

CURSIVE ITALIC

*All letters written in one stroke unless otherwise indicated. All letters start at the top except lowercase **d** and **e**.*

Aa Bb Cc Dd Ee Ff Gg
ana bnb cnc dnd ene fnf gng
                    or ene

Hh Ii Jj Kk Ll Mm
            or k
hnh ini jnj knk lnl mnm
            or knk   or mnm

Nn Oo Pp Qq Rr Ss Tt
nnn ono pnp qnq rnr sns tnt
or nnn   or rnr or sns

Uu Vv Ww Xx Yy Zz
unu vnv wnw xnx yny znz
                or xnx

INTRODUCTION TO GETTY-DUBAY™ ITALIC HANDWRITING

Book G is the seventh of seven workbooks in the *Getty-Dubay™ Italic Handwriting Series* and provides an introduction or review of basic and cursive italic. It is recommended for sixth grade and beyond, including adults.

Italic handwriting is a modern system based on sixteenth century letterforms that first developed in Italy and were later used in England and Europe. Italic provides all writers with letter shapes that are highly suited to a rapid and legible handwriting. Italic is also an art form when written as formal calligraphy. The word calligraphy, from the Greek *kalli* (beautiful) and *graphia* (writing), generally refers to letters carefully handwritten with a monoline or broad edged writing instrument. Italic calligraphy is one type of formal hand lettering. Edged pen italic is introduced in Part Three, pages 41-55.

Writing is a system of conventional signs; at any particular point in time, those using the system must be able to recognize the symbols and what they signify. The history of written symbols throughout the ages presents a fascinating story, and the writing practice in this book incorporates a brief history of our writing heritage. In addition, the historical development of each letter is included as cursive capitals are introduced.

We write for different occasions. Formal writing may encompass invitations, thank you notes, signs, posters and maps. Informal writing may include quickly written notes, letters to friends and all types of rough drafts. Fast writing may incorporate rapidly written reminders, personal notes and lists.

> Certainly
> THE ART OF WRITING
> is the most miraculous
> of all things   CARLYLE
> man has devised.
>
> BASIC ITALIC HANDWRITING, pp 1-14
>
> The history of writing is,
> in a way,
> the history
> of the human race...
> FREDERICK W. GOUDY
>
> CURSIVE ITALIC-EDGED PEN, pp 41-49
>
> Handwriting
> is a system of movements
> involving touch.
> ALFRED FAIRBANK
>
> CURSIVE ITALIC HANDWRITING, pp 15-40
>
> CALLIGRAPHY
> grasps the mind
> and makes the writing
> come alive
> LLOYD J. REYNOLDS
>
> ITALIC CALLIGRAPHY-EDGED PEN, pp 47, 49

A series of timed writings is provided to increase writing speed.

The writing process includes information regarding shape, stroke sequence, slope, size, spacing and speed. Further letter and join descriptions and assessment questions are found in the *Getty-Dubay™ Italic Handwriting Series Instruction Manual*. This Fourth Edition of Book G includes letter join options and lift options for students to consider.

Do write in this book! It is suggested you trace the model letters, then copy them in the space provided. Tracing provides an awareness of finger and hand movements which may improve manual ability.

Self-assessment is the key to improvement. The Getty-Dubay™ method enables you to monitor your own progress. STEP 1: You are asked to LOOK at your writing and affirm your best. STEP 2: You are asked to PLAN what needs to be improved and how to accomplish this. STEP 3: You are asked to put the plan into PRACTICE. This LOOK, PLAN, PRACTICE format introduces self-assessment skills applicable to all learning situations.

Additional writing aids: Getty-Dubay™ Italic Handwriting Series Desk Strips, Wall Charts and Blackline Masters are described in the Instruction Manual.

The enjoyment of good handwriting is shared by both the writer and the reader. Even in this electronic age, handwriting is a lifelong skill—good handwriting is a lifelong joy.

For more information: www.handwritingsuccess.com

NB: Source for origins of the alphabet: *Ancient Writing & Its Influence*, Berthold Ullman.

GETTY-DUBAY™ ITALIC HANDWRITING REMINDERS

PENCIL HOLD
Use a soft lead pencil (#1 or #2) with an eraser. Hold the pencil with the thumb and index finger, resting on the middle finger. The upper part of the pencil rests near the large knuckle.

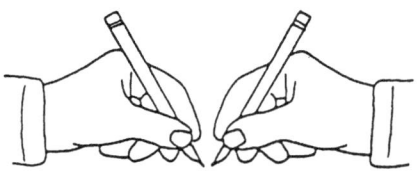
REGULAR HOLD

Hold the pencil firmly and lightly. AVOID pinching. To relax your hand, tap the index finger on the pencil three times.

Problem grips such as the 'thumb wrap' (thumb doesn't touch pencil) and the 'death grip' (very tight pencil hold) make it difficult to use the hand's small muscles. To relieve these problems, try this alternative pencil hold.

ALTERNATIVE HOLD

Place the pencil between the index finger and the middle finger. The pencil rests between the index and middle fingers by the large knuckles. Hold the pencil in the regular way at the tips of the fingers.

PAPER POSITION

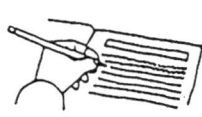

LEFT-HANDED
If you are left-handed and write with the wrist below the line of writing, turn the paper clockwise so it is slanted to the right as illustrated. If you are left-handed and write with a "hook" with the wrist above the line of writing, turn the paper counter-clockwise so it is slanted to the left as illustrated. (Similar to the right-handed position)

RIGHT-HANDED
If you are right-handed turn the paper counter-clockwise so it is slanted to the left as illustrated.

POSTURE

Rest your feet flat on the floor and keep your back comfortably straight without slumping. Rest your forearms on the desk. Hold the workbook or paper with your non-writing hand so that the writing area is centered in front of you.

LINED PAPER CHOICES
The following choices for lined paper may be used when instructions say use lined paper for practice.

1. Lines 5mm body height on page 61 may be duplicated. These lines can also be used as guidelines under a sheet of unlined paper. Fasten with paper clips.

2. Lines 4 mm body height on page 62 may be duplicated. These lines can also be used as a line guide under a sheet of unlined paper. See INSTRUCTION MANUAL pp. 103-104 for lines with capital height.

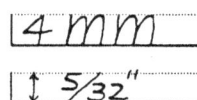

3. Some school paper has a solid baseline and a dotted waistline. Use paper with a body height of 6mm (¼") or 5mm (³⁄₁₆").

4. Some school paper has only baselines. Use paper with lines 12mm (½") or 10mm (³⁄₈") apart.

5. Use wide-ruled notebook paper with a space of about 9 mm (³⁄₈") between lines, or college ruled notebook paper 7.5mm (⁵⁄₁₆") between lines. Create your own waistline by lining up two sheets of notebook paper and shifting one down half a space. The faint line showing through will serve as a waistline.

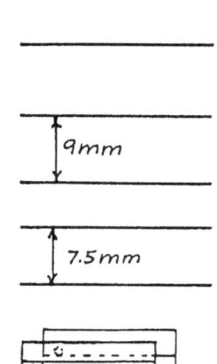

Getty-Dubay™ Italic Handwriting Reminders

VOCABULARY

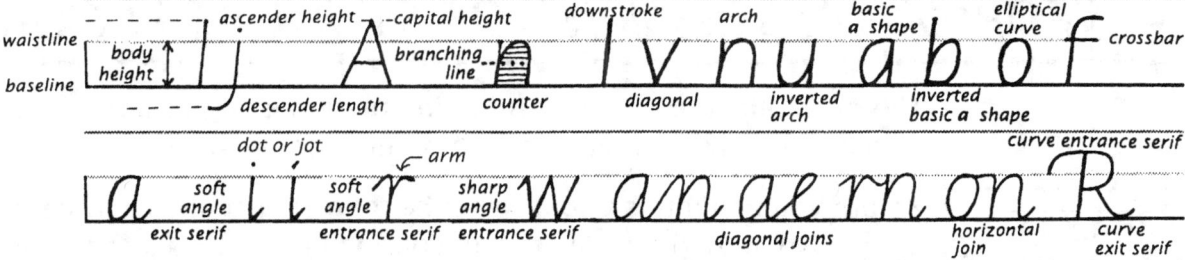

STROKES

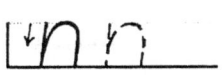

Basic italic letters all start at the top and go down or over (horizontal), except **d** and **e**. (**d** starts at the waistline and **e** starts at the center of the body height.) Follow the direction of the arrow. Letters are written in one stroke unless otherwise indicated.

Trace the dotted line model, then copy model in space provided. If needed, trace solid line model.

LETTER ASSESSMENT

SHAPE:
Basic italic lowercase letters are divided into eight families according to shape. Basic italic capitals are divided into three width groups. Cursive italic lowercase joins are divided into eight join groups.

SIZE:
Letters are written with a consistent body height. Capitals, ascenders and descenders are written one and a half times the body height.

SLOPE:
The models are written with a 5° letter slope. A consistent slope is an important part of good handwriting. For individual slope choices see *Slope Guidelines*, page 40. See 5° slope page 60.

SPACING:
Letters are written close together within words. Joins are natural spacers in cursive italic; when lifts occur, keep letters close together. Spacing between words is the width of an **n** in basic and cursive italic. See *Spacing Guidelines*, page 40.

SPEED:
Write at a comfortable rate of speed. To increase the speed of writing use the *Timed Writing*, p 38. NOTE: See *OPTIONS*, page 39.

GOAL
To write legible, neat handwriting.

IMPROVEMENT
Assessment is the key to improving your handwriting. Follow this improvement method as you learn basic and cursive italic handwriting.

- **LOOK** at your writing. ✏ Circle your best letter or join. Answer question about strokes, shape, size, spacing, or slope.

- **PLAN** how to make your writing look more like the model. Pick the letter or join that needs work. Compare with the model.

- **PRACTICE** the letter or join that needs work. Write on the lines provided and on lined paper.

- ★ Give yourself a star at the top of the page when you see you have made an improvement.

NOTE: See INSTRUCTION MANUAL, Assessment, pp. 54-68.

Getty-Dubay™ Pre-test/Post-test

INFORMAL ASSESSMENT OF STUDENT PROGRESS

The main purpose of handwriting instruction is to promote legibility so that we can communicate with others and ourselves.

PRE-TEST Before you begin this book, write the following sentence in your everyday handwriting. Also write your name, address and today's date.

A quick brown fox jumps over the lazy dog.

Write the sentence.

Name

Address

City, State

Today's date

POST-TEST After you have completed this workbook, write the following sentence in cursive italic. Also write your name, address and today's date in cursive italic.

A quick brown fox jumps over the lazy dog.

Write the sentence.

Name

Address

City, State

Today's date

ASSESSMENT
- SHAPE: Each letter is similar to the models in the workbook.
- SIZE: Similar letters are the same height (for example: aec, dhk, gpy). Capital letters and lowercase letters with ascenders are the same height.
- SLOPE: Letters have a consistent letter slope (between 5° – 15°).
- SPACING: Letters within words are closely spaced. Spaces between words are the width of **n**.
- SPEED: Words are written fluently at a comfortable speed.

Getty-Dubay™ Italic Handwriting Series · Book G © 2013 Getty-Dubay

·abcdefghijklmnopqrstuvwxyz·

PART ONE

Getty-Dubay™
Basic Italic
& Numerals

Lowercase
Capitals
Numerals
Writing Practice
Handwriting Tips

·abcdefghijklmnopqrstuvwxyz·

GETTY-DUBAY™ BASIC ITALIC LOWERCASE FAMILIES

i j l · k or k v w x z · h m n r · u y · a d g q · b p · o e c s · f t
FAMILY 1   2   3   4   5   6   7   8

These letter families are presented according to similar letter shapes. The 9mm body height will help you focus on the letter shapes, pencil/pen hold and hand movements before moving to a smaller, more natural letter size.

Write all letters in one stroke without lifting your pencil/pen unless otherwise indicated. Trace each letter, then write your own in the space provided. Take note of letter families and shapes as you practice.

FAMILY 1 — straight line downstroke (see vocabulary, p. vii)

ascender height
waistline
branching line — 9mm body height
baseline
descender length

i i i   j j j   l l l

FAMILY 2 — diagonal strokes

k k or k k   v v   w w   x x   z z

cross x at branching line or slightly above

k   k   v   w   x   z

FAMILY 3 — arch

h h   m m   n n   r r

branching line

form arch by retracing downstroke back up to the branching line, then curve upward to the right

slightly bend down arm of r

h   m   n   r

FAMILY 4 — inverted arch

u u   y y   u   y

WRITING PRACTICE · keep letters close together within words

kiwi   hurry

9mm

Getty-Dubay™ Basic Italic Lowercase Families

LOWERCASE FAMILIES, continued

FAMILY 5 basic *a* shape

begin horizontally
abrupt curve

a a   d d   g g   q q

a   d   g   q

FAMILY 6 inverted basic *a* shape

FAMILY 7 elliptical curve

b b   p p

o o   e e

begin e at branching line   alternate 2-stroke e:

b   p

o   e

FAMILY 7, continued

FAMILY 8 crossbar

c c   s s

f f   t t

c   s

f   t

WRITING PRACTICE · a pangram (a sentence containing all 26 letters of our alphabet)

a quick brown fox

a

jumps over the lazy dog

j

9mm

Practice words and sentences on notebook paper, writing a space high. See pp. 53-55 for additional pangrams.

GETTY-DUBAY™ BASIC ITALIC LOWERCASE FAMILIES

i j l · k or k v w x z · h m n r · u y · a d g q · b p · o e c s · f t
FAMILY 1   2   3   4   5   6   7   8

All letters are written in one stroke with no pencil/pen lift unless otherwise indicated.

FAMILY 1 — i j l

i i i i   j j j j   l l l l

RELAX Exhale on downstroke. This may help you write straight lines.

Trace & copy line above. Fill each line on the page.

i   j   l

FAMILY 2 — k v w x z

OPTION:
k k   or   k k   v v   w w   x x   z z

☐ 1 LOOK at your writing.

k   k   v   w   x   z

Trace and write: will will

FAMILY 3 — h m n r

h h   m m   n n   r r

✏ Circle your best m.

h   m   n   r

☐ 2 PLAN which letters need work. How will you make them look more like the models?

mix mix   rim rim

FAMILY 4 — u y

u u   y y

· PICTURE WRITING ·

u   y

FAMILY 5 — a d g q

a a a   d d d

NOTE: Close up the top of a, d, g and q.

a   d

☐ 3 PRACTICE on notebook paper the letters that need more work.

g g g   q q q

g   q

adding a

As far as we know, about 28,000 BCE people began painting pictures on the walls of the caves. Paintings of bison, rhinoceroses, horses and bulls have been found in Spain and France. Early paintings and drawings show animals in action— the beginning of storytelling.

FAMILY 6 — b p

b b   p p   bumpy

b   p   b

5mm

SELF-ASSESSMENT: Do your letters slope in the same direction?   bumpy

Getty-Dubay™ Italic Handwriting Series · Book G

Getty-Dubay™ Basic Italic Lowercase

FAMILY 7
o e c s

o o o   e e e   OPTION: or e e e
overlap stroke 2 / over stroke 1

2-stroke e:
See page 24,
cursive join 3.

Trace & copy the line above.

o   e   e

NOTE: Close up the top of o.

c c c   s s s

Circle your best o, e, c, & s.

c   s

AMERICAN INDIAN SIGNS

bear tracks, mountains, rain clouds, tepee (tipi), lightning

Before alphabets were developed, many peoples of the world used pictures to tell stories and to send messages and instructions.

FAMILY 8
f t

f f f   t t t

t is a short letter!

f   t

ocean   tepee   clouds   mountains

ocean

PANGRAM   a quick brown fox jumps over the lazy dog

a

SHAPE SLOPE SPACING STROKES

Lowercase italic is based on the elliptical*

Trace & copy this paragraph.

i

shape. The letters slope slightly to the

The diagonal lines at the right are sloped 5° to the right. Slope your writing 0°–15° to the right. Be consistent.

right and are closely spaced. Twenty

Tracing letters gives you the feel of the letters and the correct spacing within and between words.

of the letters are written in one stroke.

2-STROKE LETTERS   f f   i i   j j   k k   t t   x x

5mm

*elliptical: shaped like an ellipse—an oval having both ends alike: O

GETTY-DUBAY™ BASIC ITALIC CAPITALS

These capital families are presented according to similar letter widths.

CDGOQ · MW · AHKNTUVXYZ · EFILBPRSJ
WIDE · WIDEST · MEDIUM · NARROW

Trace and copy. Fill each line. (Capitals are 1½ times the body height of lowercase letters.)

WIDE — C C D D G G O O Q Q
These letters are about as wide as they are tall.

WIDEST — M M W W
Letters are wider than they are tall.

· SUMERIAN PICTOGRAMS ·

ox — sun — house — stand go (foot) (ideogram)

The most ancient system of writing we know of was used by the Sumerians who lived in Mesopotamia before 4,000 BCE.

At first, like other cultures, they drew objects simply. Then, as shown above, the picture became a symbol of the object rather than the object itself. These symbols are called pictograms.

Symbols which represent ideas, like "day," "time," "go," "stand," are called ideograms.

MEDIUM — A A H H K K / N N T T U U
Letters are about ⅘ as wide as they are tall.

Do you know we read and write capitals only about 2% of the time? — V V X X Y Y Z Z

NARROW — E E F F I I L L
NOTE: Stroke 3 lower than 3 on E   I is the narrowest capital
Letters are about ½ as wide as they are tall.
B B P P R R or R R S S J J or J J
for rapid writing

CAPITAL PRACTICE — MESOPOTAMIA · 4,000 BCE

height of caps — M

5mm

LARGE & SMALL BASIC ITALIC CAPITAL LETTERS

In addition to using capital letters (caps) with lowercase letters, plain caps may be used for headings, titles, posters, banners, addresses, abbreviations, certificates and other uses.

LARGE CAPS

MEETING · 4 P.M. TODAY · ROOM 2
— Cap height line   write P.M. shorter

notice of meeting

M

certificate title

HANDWRITING AWARD

Visualize the height of caps. They are 1½ times the body height.

H

SMALL CAPS

A B C D E F G H I J or J K L M N

Small caps may be written wider than large caps.

A

O P Q R or R S T U V W X Y & Z
                                    FROM LATIN ET: AND

O

CAP PRACTICE

LARGE CAPS AND SMALL CAPS MAY BE USED SEPARATELY OR TOGETHER

· CUNEIFORM WRITING ·

About 2500 BCE

water — dwelling place (house) — mountain

About 1300 BCE

B — G — P — stylus (writing tool)

Periods may or may not be used with many abbreviations.

RSVP · P.S. · A.M. P.M.
write a.m. and p.m. in lowercase unless using all caps

R

(cuneiform - from Latin: *cuneus* - wedge, *forma* - shape)

The Sumerians generally wrote on damp clay tablets. Mistakes could be easily smoothed out, but it was difficult to draw curves or circles in the clay. So the scribes began using a wedge-shaped tool of wood, bone or metal which they pressed in the clay.

The use of cuneiform spread to other cultures, among them, Persians, Babylonians and Hittites.

The script finally appeared in one form as a genuine alphabet of 30 symbols in the ancient city of Ugarit in northern Syria.

address

1345 NW CAPITAL

1

State and zip code should be written on the same line on envelopes.

PORTLAND OR 97286

P

MIXED CAPS

THE STORY OF HANDWRITING
by Alfred Fairbank · New York: Watson-Guptil, 1970

T

5mm
E 1½ times body height

✏ Are your large caps 1½ times the body height of lowercase letters?

© 2013 Getty-Dubay   7   Getty-Dubay™ Italic Handwriting Series · Book G

GETTY-DUBAY™ NUMERALS

The word NUMBER stands for an idea—how many objects in a certain group.
The word NUMERAL describes the symbol we use for the number idea.

Just as the first writing happened long after people began speaking, writing numerals to represent numbers came long after people began counting. The earliest numerals known were marks on stones and notices in sticks.

About 3,400 BCE, the Egyptians developed a written number system using hieroglyphics, as shown:

One problem with the Egyptian system and those of the Greeks and the Romans is that none of them had a symbol to represent zero, "not any." In most early systems, people formed numerals by repeating a few basic symbols, then adding their values.

The numerals we use most likely came by way of Arabia from a starting point in India. The Indians had a superior system — a base of ten and symbols for each number from one to nine. This was about 300 BCE. The use of the numeral zero we know today probably first took hold in India in the 5th century CE. Later, these numerals arrived in Europe, by way of Spain, and were developed into the system that is used in most parts of the world today.

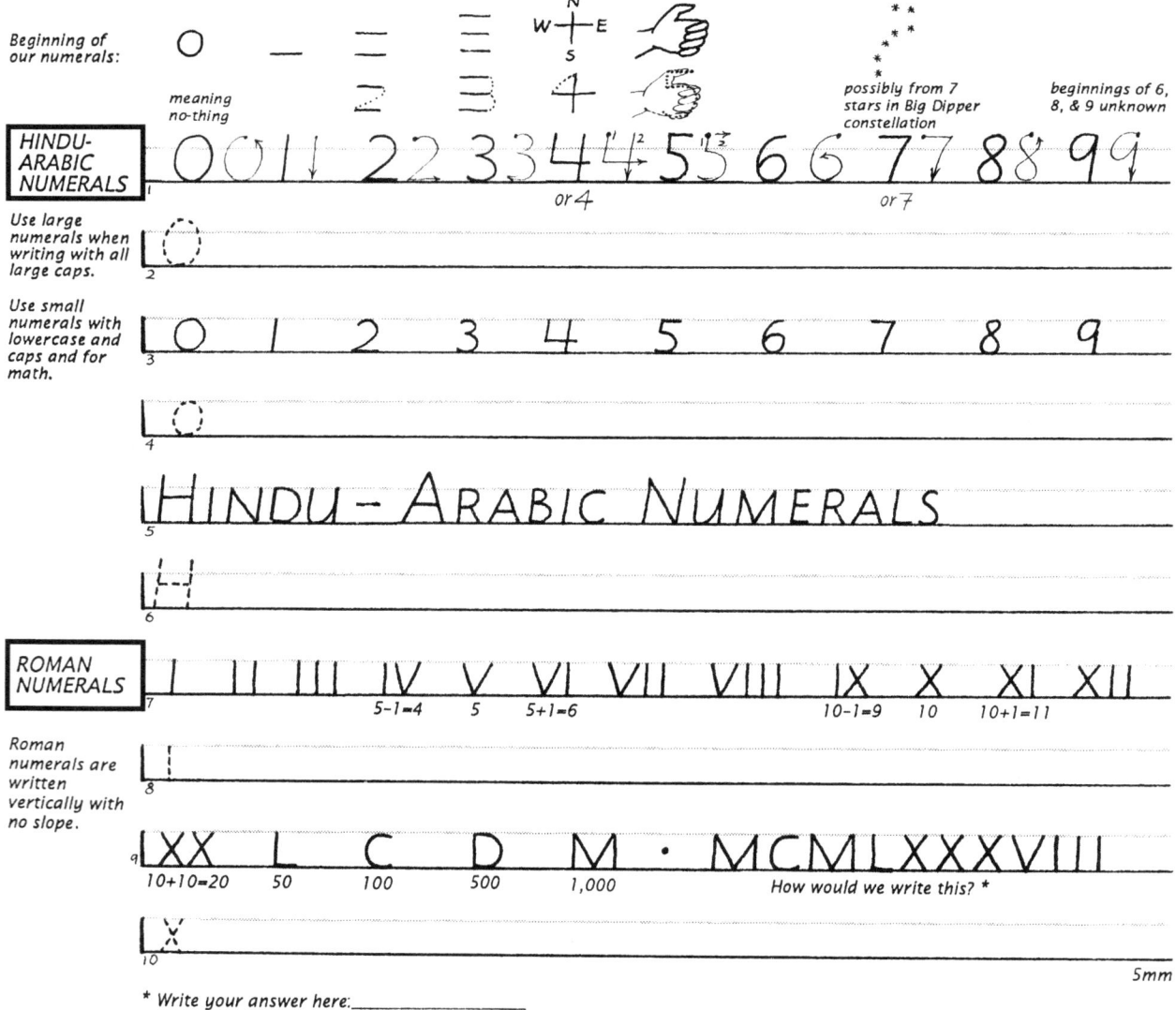

* Write your answer here: _____

Getty-Dubay™ Italic Handwriting Series · Book G
© 2013 Getty-Dubay

Getty-Dubay™ Numerals

Address
1456 N.W. Lakeview Drive

Note use of small numerals and small caps.
Portland OR 97238-1027

Trace & copy lines above.

Write your own address,

and city, state & zip:

Phone no., abbr. date, height or length.
(123) 456-7890   3/20/94   5' 7"
area code   prefix   number

Money amounts and metric system abbreviations.
$15.27   98¢   6 cm   124 kg   539 km
centimeters   kilograms   kilometers

Time and temperature
8:30 a.m.   12:45 p.m.   74°F   30°C
ante-meridian - before noon   post-meridian - after noon

Usually we write them with small numerals, but write these large. Which do you prefer?

Fractions
½   4⅔   8¾   7⅞   1¹⁵⁄₁₆

Punctuation
. , ' ? ! " " - —
apos-   hyphen dash
trophe

Punctuation adds meaning & expression to written words.

Punctuation and other symbols
( ) ¢ $ @ * / & &
parentheses   'at'   slant   ampersands
                      or slash Latin ET 'and'

5mm

CARTOUCHE OF TUTANKHAMUN
A cartouche represents a looped rope indicating the king was ruler of all that the sun encircled.

· EGYPTIAN WRITING ·
3,000 BCE – 400 CE

Of the three kinds of ancient writing scripts used in Egypt, hieroglyphic is the oldest.* ("hieroglyphic" – sacred engraved writing)

At first, they used only pictograms, then idea pictures – ideograms. Finally they used these to spell words.** Egyptians wrote both horizontally ⇌ and vertically. ↓

CARTOUCHE OF CLEOPATRA

TRANSLATION:
K L E O P A T R A   divine female

Above, you can see that all but two symbols were used to spell Cleopatra. The other two symbols are ideograms.

The Egyptians continued to mix their systems rather than using a single system. (At times we also use more than one system: EXIT)

* Only one is mentioned here.
** These then became phonograms. (A phonogram is a symbol that stands for a single speech sound.)

GETTY-DUBAY™ BASIC ITALIC WRITING PRACTICE

TRACE AND COPY

If this book is your first experience writing italic, continue to trace the models before copying.

We use the 26 letters of our alphabet
w
daily in reading and writing, but seldom
d
are we aware of their beginnings.

The body height is now 1mm less (4mm) than on previous pages.

OPTION:

You may connect fr and fi.

The word ALPHABET
t
comes from the Greek

names of the first two

letters of their alpha-

bet, ALPHA and BETA.

· THE PHOENICIAN ALPHABET ·
about 2,000 BCE

Many historians feel we can thank the Phoenicians for the beginning of our alphabet. It is thought that their alphabet of 22 letters* was developed from Egyptian hieroglyphs. The Phoenicians used all of their symbols as consonants.

Can you translate this?**

All of those who came in touch with the Phoenicians borrowed their alphabet and changed it to suit their own needs.

[1] **LOOK** at your writing.

[2] **PLAN** which letters need work. How will you make them look more like the models?

Some time before 1,300 BCE, the Phoeni-
s
cian alphabet was brought to Greece.

[3] **PRACTICE** on notebook paper the letters that need more work.

The Greeks added vowels to the alphabet.

SELF-ASSESSMENT: Are you beginning ā ā ḡ q̄ c̄ s̄ with a horizontal line?
Are you ending b p with a horizontal line?

4mm

* ⊕ (th) and ƕ (ts) complete the 22 symbols. ** The Phoenicians wrote from right to left.

Getty-Dubay™ Italic Handwriting Series · Book G   © 2013 Getty-Dubay

Getty-Dubay™ Basic Italic

> The Greeks also helped determine the direction of our writing. The Phoenicians generally wrote from right to left, and early Greek writing followed this same pattern.

You may cross ft and tt in one stroke. It's faster!

1. LOOK at your writing.
2. PLAN which letters need work. How will you make them look more like the models?
3. PRACTICE on notebook paper the letters that need more work.

> Then the Greeks began writing in both directions as the oxen plowed the fields.* By the 5th century BCE they had changed to our present way, from left to right.

CHECKLIST
___ shape
___ size
___ slope
___ spacing

4mm

· GREEK WRITING ·

The Greeks cut letters in stone, scratched letters in clay, wrote on papyrus and on slabs of wood and ivory coated with wax that was stained black. A metal or bone stylus was used to inscribe letters on the wax tablets.

ΑΚΑΔΗΜΙΑ (ACADEMY)
ΣΧΟΛΗ (SCHOOL)
ΠΟΙΗΤΗΣ (POET)

wax tablet   stylus

Boustrophedon Writing*

SOMEGREEKWRITINGWASWRI
TTENASTHEOXENPLOWEDTHE
LANDMANYLETTERSHADTOB
EREVERSEDASIHAVEDONEHER
EANDTHEGREEKSALSOWROTEL
IKETHISWITHOUTSPACESBET
WEENWORDSANDWITHOUT
ANYPUNCTUATIONMARKS

*boustrophedon: bi-directional writing, "ox-turning" or "as the ox plows"

SELF-ASSESSMENT: Are you leaving about the width of *n* between words?   tor the

Use basic italic for maps, signs, posters, banners - any time you want something easily read at a distance.

NOTE: In this book, all the writing for student practice and historic notes, such as this map, was written by hand.

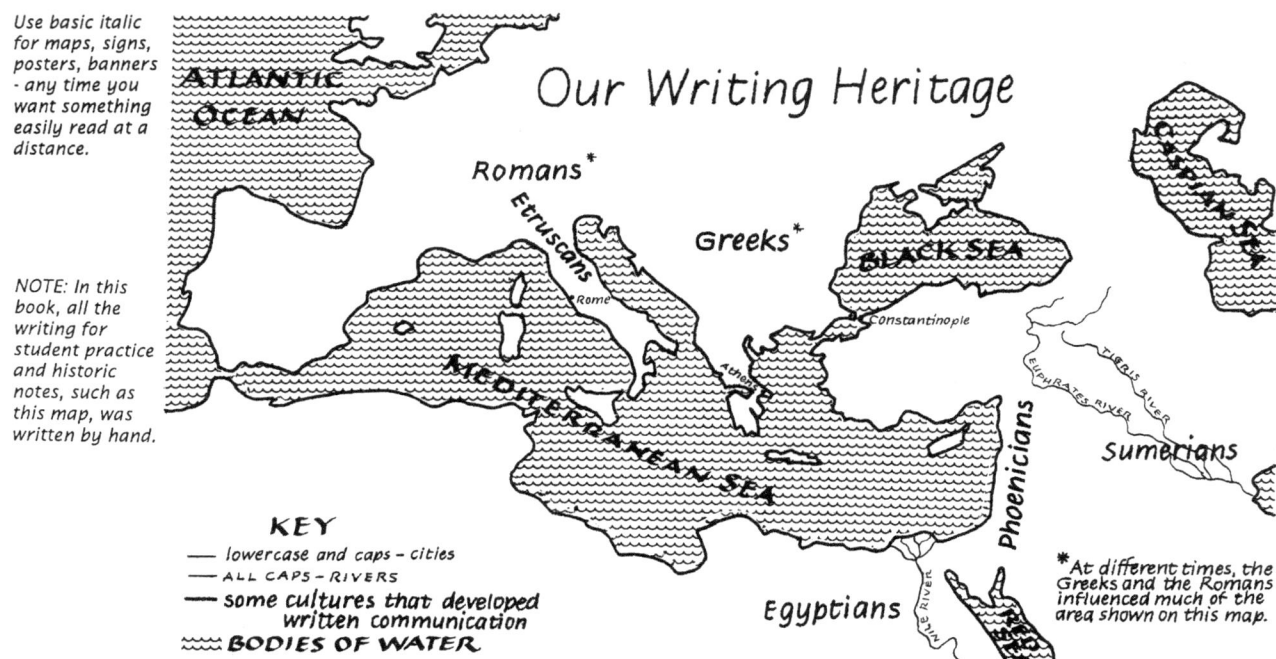

Our Writing Heritage

ATLANTIC OCEAN
Romans*
Etruscans
Rome
Greeks*
BLACK SEA
CASPIAN SEA
Constantinople
Athens
MEDITERRANEAN SEA
TIGRIS RIVER
EUPHRATES RIVER
Sumerians
Phoenicians
Egyptians
NILE RIVER
RED SEA
KEY
lowercase and caps - cities
ALL CAPS - RIVERS
some cultures that developed written communication
BODIES OF WATER
*At different times, the Greeks and the Romans influenced much of the area shown on this map.

WRITING LINES: You may reproduce the lines on pages 61-62 for writing practice, or use them underneath as guidelines when writing on plain paper. Choose the writing size which is most comfortable for you—5mm or 4mm.

On this page, the baselines 1-14 are spaced similarly to wide-ruled notebook paper:

by
they
the

1 The Etruscans acquired the alphabet
2 from the Greeks. In turn, the alphabet
3 was further developed by the Romans.
4
5
6

College ruled:

by
they
the

7
8 Today we use
9 all 23 of the
10 Roman letters.**
11
12
13
14

4mm

** The letters j, u and w were added later.

· THE ETRUSCANS ·
1,000–200 BCE

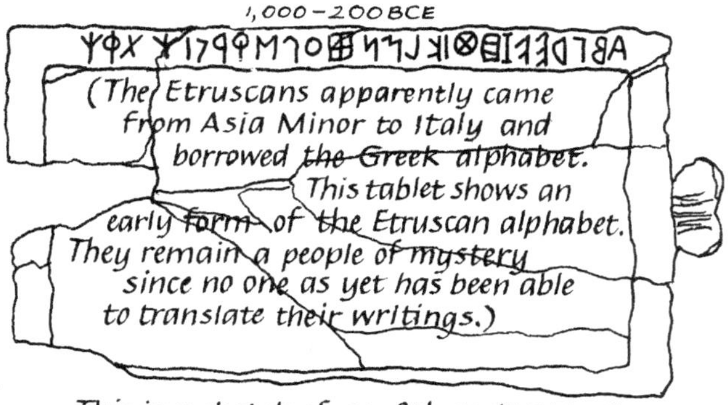
(The Etruscans apparently came from Asia Minor to Italy and borrowed ~~the Greek alphabet~~.
This tablet shows an early ~~form~~ of the Etruscan alphabet.
They remain a people of ~~mystery~~ since no one as yet has been able to translate their writings.)

This is a sketch of an 8th century BCE Etruscan writing tablet. It is called the MARSILIANA ABECEDARIUM.

NOTE: The Etruscans wrote from right to left.

Are your letters close together within words? Trace the models for help.

GETTY-DUBAY™ HANDWRITING TIPS

To alleviate pinching your writing tool, tap your finger three times. The way your finger rests on the tool is the way you should hold it as you write. Tap periodically!

•

Note that this is handwriting—not finger or arm writing. Move from the wrist with minimal finger movement. Write an "m" arcade and a "u" arcade for practice:

arch mmm mmm mmm mmm
counter

uuuu uuuu uuuu uuuu

Write these arcades quickly in a relaxed manner. Practicing the arcade in spare moments—as you wait for an appointment, as you talk on the phone—will help you gain rhythm in your writing.

•

The cursive handwriting many of us learned in school has loops in ascenders and descenders that often cause illegibility.

fill *fill*
hill *hill*

looped cursive   cursive italic

As you learn cursive italic, begin eliminating the loops in the ascenders and descenders of your own handwriting if you currently use them.

We read letters from the top— can you read these two words?

AMERICA
VICTORIA

We read the tops of lower-case letters at the waist line area. Italic letters are easily read because they are loop free.

•

Check the interior and exterior counters of families 5 and 6:

interior counter
a d g q
exterior counter

b p ⊘ ⊘   basic *a* shape and inverted basic *a* shape

NOTE: The basic *a* shape and the inverted basic *a* shape have identical counters as do the arch: n ⌂ and the inverted arch: u ⌂

Maintaining consistent counters of these letters will help you achieve a harmonious rhythmic hand. Practice the following words:

adage   bundle

pique   pod   NOTE: Invert (rotate) "pod." Are counters consistent?

•

Establish your own waistline when using notebook paper. A consistent body height (x height) is one of the essential characteristics of legibility. (See SIZE GUIDE, p.60)

NOTE: Pages 13 & 14 are handwritten as are all letter models throughout this book.

HANDWRITING TIPS, continued

Look carefully at the letter shapes. It's very easy to say, "I know the shape of A—I've written it all my life." However, you may have overlooked the actual shape of the letter A.

Ways to improve your ability to see shapes: First, look at the negative spaces—the counters of the letters. Draw only the counter shapes and you'll see letters in a new way, for example:

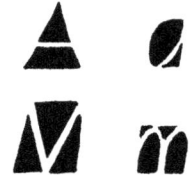

Second, look at letter shapes upside down. It may be exasperating to read, but it is an ideal way to see the shapes of letters.

Look at your own handwriting upside down. (shown upside down)

"In copying signatures, forgers turn the originals upside down to see the exact shapes of the letters more clearly."[1]

•

Let the speed of your writing suit the task, but don't sacrifice legibility for speed. You and others must be able to read it.

•

ONE WAY TO PRACTICE:

1. Trace model.
2. Write letter 3 times.
3. Compare your letter with model.
   Check: a. letter slope
           b. letter width
           c. letter counter
4. Retrace model.
5. Adjust your letter as needed.
6. Rewrite letter alternating with another letter.
7. Evaluate your writing.
8. Close your eyes and write the letter.

P A T I E N C E

•

If you write a backhand with letters sloping to the left, you can change your letter slope by shifting your paper. There is no need to alter the way you hold your writing tool. It is generally easier to read letters that are vertical or that slope to the right. Whether you are left-handed or righthanded, experiment with paper position.

•

After you complete this book, use italic for all of your handwriting at home and at work. As you journey through this book, begin addressing envelopes for practice. Then start writing letters to friends. Many of us feel we have little time to write letters, but it is a wonderful way to practice your italic and also keep in touch with friends. And once in a-while at the end of a busy day, you may return home and find a reply in your own mailbox.

•

1. Betty Edwards. DRAWING ON THE RIGHT SIDE OF THE BRAIN. Los Angeles: J.P. Tarcher, Inc., 1979, p. 51.

abcdefghijklmnopqrstuvwxyz

PART TWO

Getty-Dubay™
Cursive Italic

Cursive Capitals
Transition to Cursive Lowercase
Eight Joins
Writing Practice
Timed Writing
Options
Guidelines

abcdefghijklmnopqrstuvwxyz

GETTY-DUBAY™ CURSIVE ITALIC CAPITALS

The Roman alphabet is derived from the Phoenician alphabet. The Greeks added vowels to the Phoenician alphabet, which, in turn, evolved from Egyptian hieroglyphs.

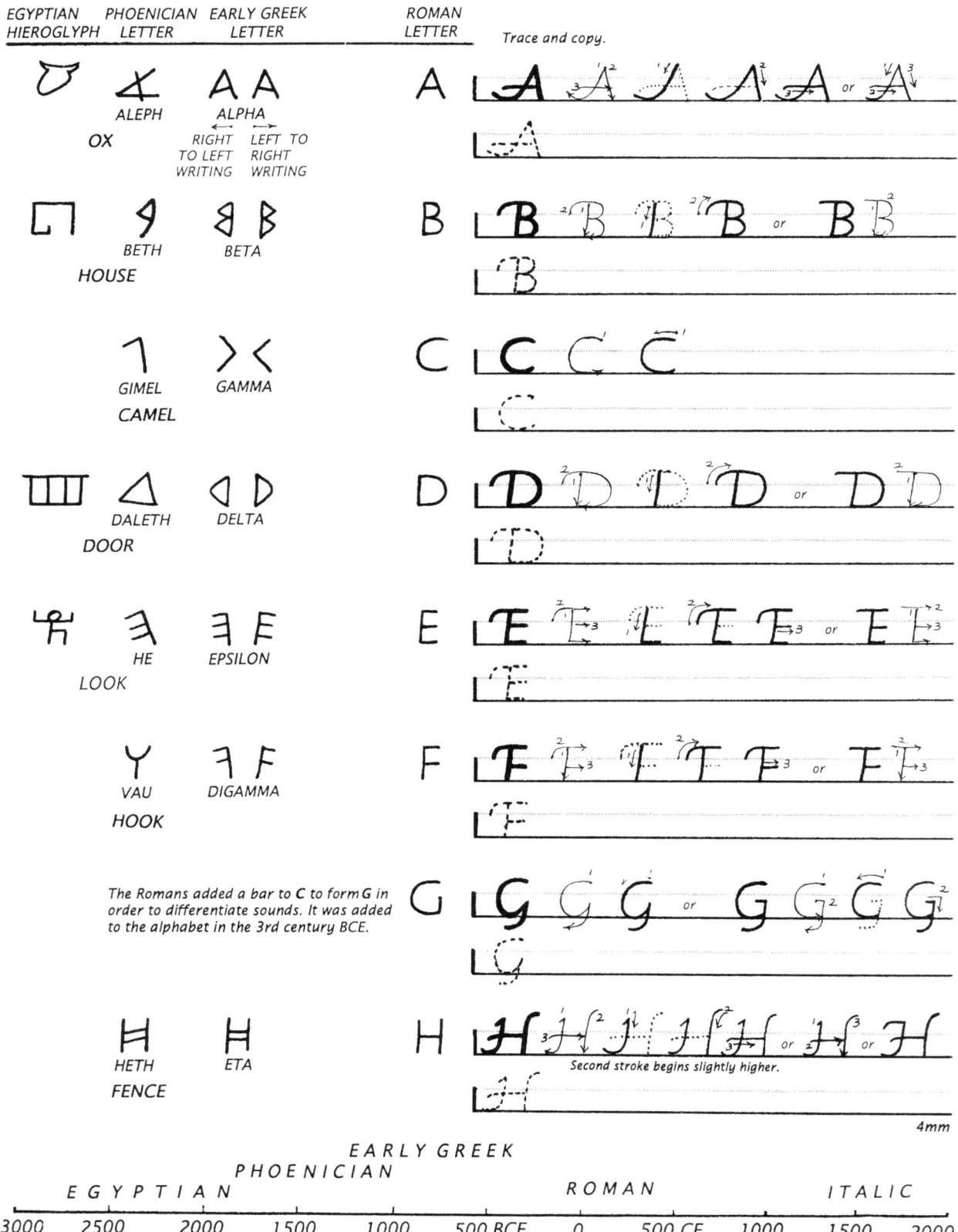

Getty-Dubay™ Cursive Italic Capitals

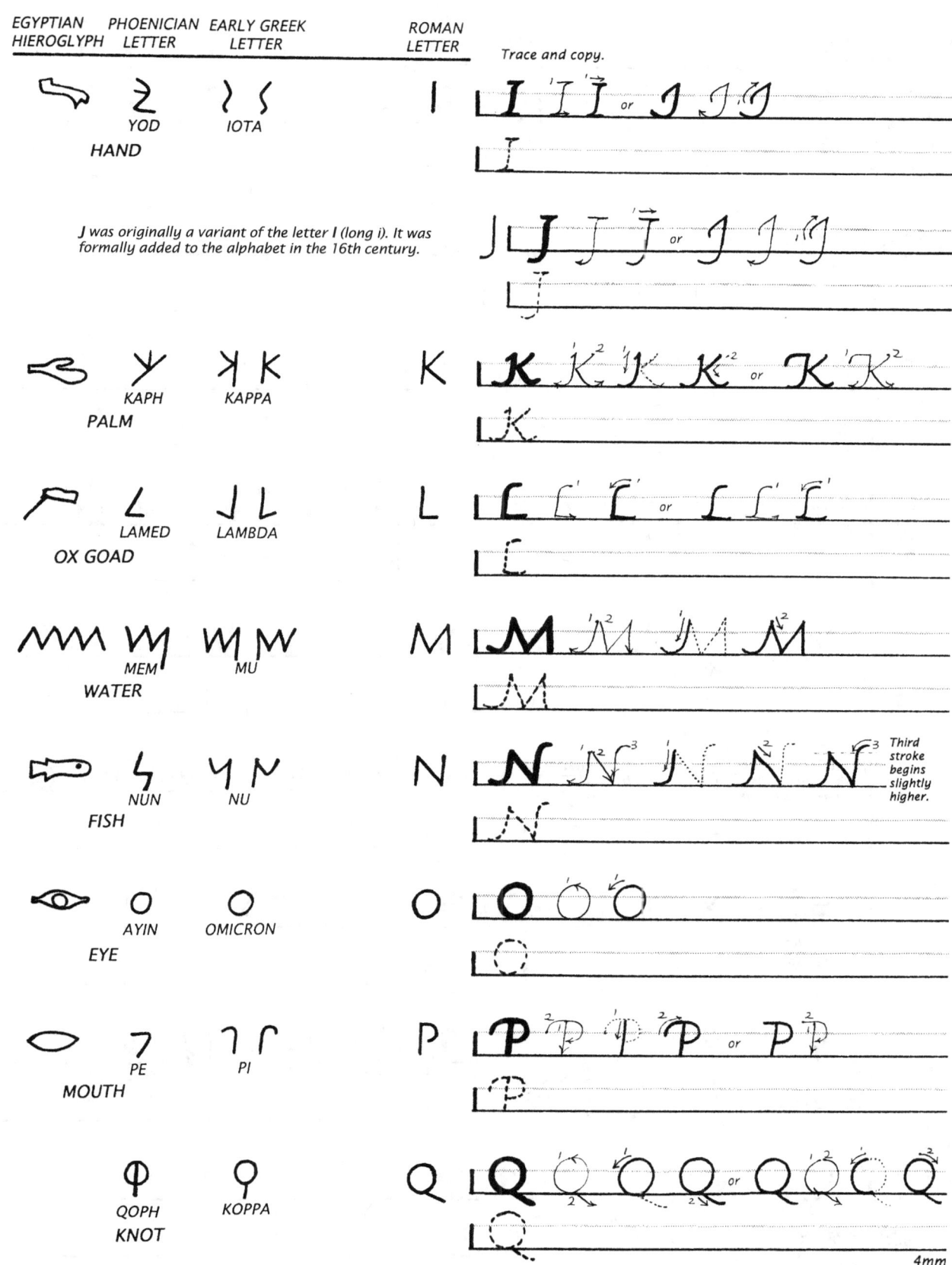

Egyptian hieroglyphs are written from top to bottom, usually right to left; also horizontally.

Phoenician letters are written horizontally, right to left, as Hebrew and Arabic are written today.

Early Greek and Roman letters are written in alternating directions, right to left, then left to right, — as a field is plowed. (See boustrophedon writing on page 11.) After about 500 BCE, the writing direction from left to right is established.

Getty-Dubay™ Cursive Italic Capitals

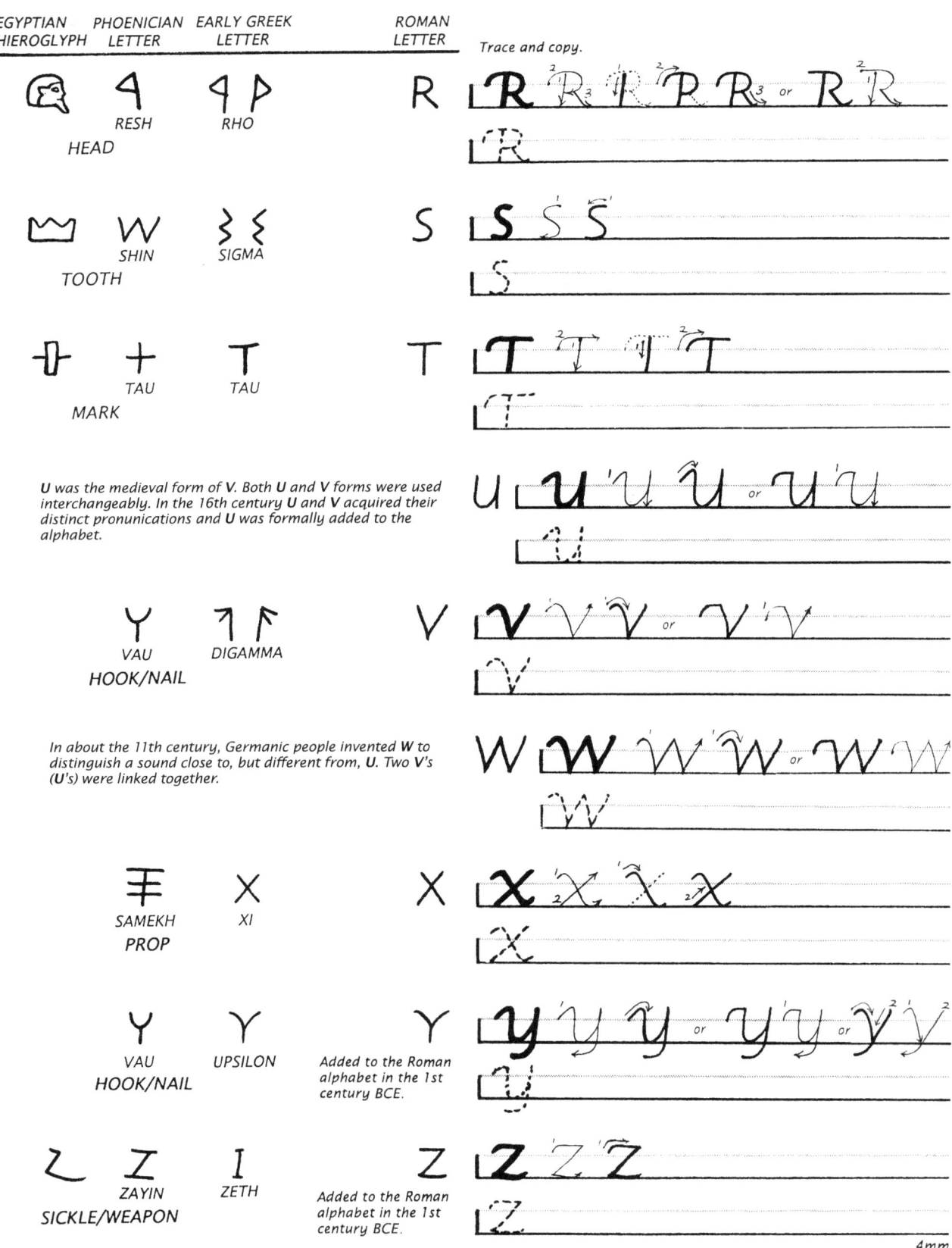

The development of the alphabet as shown is based on ANCIENT WRITING AND ITS INFLUENCE by Berthold Louis Ullman (1969 MIT Press).

NOTE: See INSTRUCTION MANUAL, Cursive Italic Capitals Description, p. 43 and Cursive Italic Capitals Assessment Questions, p. 65.

TRANSITION TO GETTY-DUBAY™ CURSIVE ITALIC

Serifs are lines added to the main strokes of a letter.
Some serifs are slightly rounded and some are sharp.

d becomes d • n becomes n • j becomes j

soft angle entrance serif
soft angle exit serif added
soft angle entrance serif and exit serif added
sharp angle entrance serif added
sharp angle entrance serif
soft angle exit serif

CURSIVE LOWERCASE: a b c d e f g h i j k l m n o p q r s t u v w x y z*

serif (ser'if): a fine line added to a letter

SOFT ANGLE EXIT SERIFS: a a d d h h i i k k or k k OPTION

Soft angle exit serif out of a, d, h, i, k, l, m, n, u and z. Also first stroke of x.

l l m m n n u u x x z z

NOTE: See below for entrance serifs for m, n & x.

ah ah ai ai ak ak al al au au

SOFT ANGLE ENTRANCE SERIFS: m m n n r r x x

Soft angle serif into n, m, r & x.

When joining keep diagonal straight.

am am an an ar ar ax ax

SHARP ANGLE ENTRANCE SERIFS: j p v w • aj aj ap ap av av aw aw

Sharp angle serif into j, p, v & w.

JOTTED I, J DESCENDER f: f f i i (OPTION) j j (OPTION)

Descender f
Dot or jot i & j.

NOTE: These letters do not have entrance or exit serifs added.

*REMAIN THE SAME: b c e g o q s t y

ROMAN WRITING

A gold brooch, the PRAENESTE FIBULA, 7th century BCE, contains the earliest known Latin inscription. It was found about 20 miles southeast of Rome.

Early Roman letterforms began with Latin inscriptions in stone and on metal. They also wrote on papyrus, wax tablets, bark & pottery. Their early letters resembled Greek & Etruscan as shown above. Later they became the capital letters we still use today.

5mm

© 2013 Getty-Dubay   Getty-Dubay™ Italic Handwriting Series · Book G

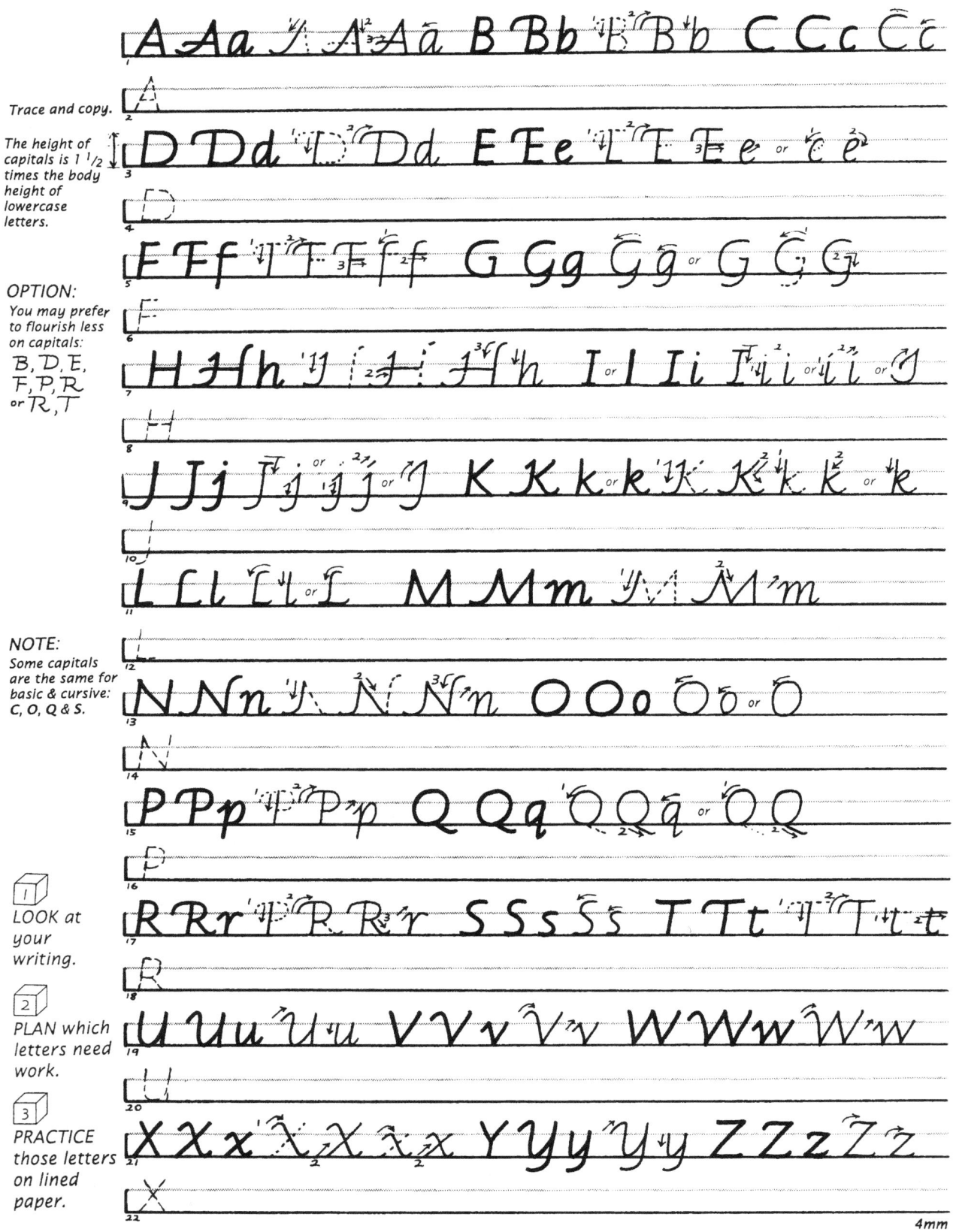

GETTY-DUBAY™ CURSIVE ITALIC LOWERCASE

JOIN 1: *an am ar ax* **DIAGONAL**
Join with a straight diagonal line, then roll over into **n, m, r, x**.

an — Trace and copy.
an cn dn en hn in kn ln mn
an
nn un zn · Ian Jan Len Ann
nn

am
am em im mm nm um · Sam
am

ar
ar cr dr er ir kr ur
ar

ax
ax ex ix ux · Max
ax

NOTE: For an optional join into n, m, r & x see page 23.

Van Dan Kim Pam
V
Cam Tim Sara

· PAPYRUS ·
diameter often 20–30 millimeters
rind removed
inner pith sliced into strips
Reeds often grow up to a height of 8 meters.
After the stalks are cut, the thin strips are laid crosswise on a flat surface in a double layer. A cloth is laid over the strips and the papyrus is beaten with a wooden mallet until the strips are matted together.

LOOK at your writing. ✏ Are you joining with a straight diagonal line? *an* (AVOID *an*)

Join 1 is used here. Dotted lines indicate Joins 2–8.

The Egyptians, Greeks and Romans used papyrus as a writing surface.

The word "paper" is derived from "papyrus."

CHECKLIST
____ shape
____ size
____ slope
____ spacing

4mm

OPTION: Join 2 into n, m, r, and x. See p. 23.

NOTE: See INSTRUCTION MANUAL, Cursive Italic Join Descriptions, pp. 46–49.
Assessment, pp. 54–68.

Getty-Dubay™ Cursive Italic Lowercase

JOIN 2: *au ay ai at aj ap av aw al ah ab ak* **DIAGONAL SWING UP** **OPTION:** *an am ar ax*

Join with a diagonal line blending into a swing-up stroke.

au ay — au ay cu cy du dy eu ey hu hy iu iy

Trace and copy. au

ki ky lu ly mu my nu ny uy zu zy

ki

ai at — ai at ci ct di dt ei et hi ht it ki kt li

ai

lt mi mt ni nt ui ut zi · Pat Mimi

lt

aj ap — aj ap ej ep ip lp mp np up · Kip

aj

av aw — av aw ev ew iv iw uv uw · Lew Liv

av

OPTION: You may prefer to round slightly the point of v and the points of w at the baseline.

av aw ev ew iv iw · Lew Liv

av

al ah — al ah cl ch dl eh il ih ll ml nl nh

CHECKLIST
___ shape
___ size
___ slope
___ spacing

al

ul uh · Sally Philip Emily Anh Vinh

ul

ab ak — ab ak ck eb ek ib ik lk nk ub uk · Tab

ab

4mm

Getty-Dubay™ Cursive Italic Lowercase

OPTION: You may prefer to join into n, m, r and x using Join 2 - Diagonal Swing Up, instead of Join 1.

an
Trace and copy.

an en in un · am em im um · Jan Jim

ar er ir ur · Sara · ax ex ix ux · Max

Van Vinh Pam Tim Mimi Tex Lux

1. LOOK at your writing.

Are your joins and letters blending halfway? *att* (AVOID *au*)

Are you joining into l, h, b and k with a single line? *al* (AVOID scoop and loop *al*)

NOTE: Join 2 is used here, including the optional join into n, m, r and x. Dotted lines indicate Joins 3-8.

The Latin word for scroll is "volumen" from which comes our word "volume."

2. PICK the joins that need work. Compare them with the models. PLAN how to make the joins look more like the models.

· SCROLL ·
A label (Latin "titulus") is attached to the end for identification.

Some scrolls are more than thirty meters in length.

Both papyrus & parchment are used in scrolls & codices.

· CODEX ·
Sheets are folded for easier storage and transporting.

3. PRACTICE those joins on lined paper.

The word "parchment" is from the Latin "pergamena"– from the city Pergamum in Greece. The earliest Greek parchment manuscripts date from the second century BCE.

Parchment, made from the skins of animals, was easier to write on than papyrus and soon became the chief writing material.

Sheep, goat, and calf skins are used for parchment.

4mm

© 2013 Getty-Dubay   23   Getty-Dubay™ Italic Handwriting Series · Book G

Getty-Dubay™ Cursive Italic Lowercase

JOIN 3: *ao* DIAGONAL START BACK
Join with a straight diagonal line, then start back into **o**.

ao | ao co do eo ho io ko lo mo no uo zo

Trace and copy. *ao*

Leo Julio Lito

☐ **LOOK**

✎ Are you joining with a straight diagonal? *ao* (AVOID *ao*)

Joins 1-3 are used here. Dotted lines indicate Joins 4-8.

The Chinese invented paper in 105 CE.

OPTION: You may prefer to join into **s** using Join 3. The top of **s** is left off using this join.   Another option: See Join 8, p. 30.

as | as cs ds es hs is ks ls ms ns us zs Luis

as

NOTE: This optional join into **s** is used in the sentence writing practice from pages 25 to 29.

OPTION: You may prefer to use a 2-stroke **e**. *e e* Join into the top of **e**. *ae ae*

ae | ae ae ce de he ie ke le me ne ue ze

ae ae

OPTION: If you prefer the 2-stroke **e**, join out of the second stroke. *en*

en | en eu el eo ee ea · Len Leo Lee Bea

AVOID *en, en*

en

Shelley
S

☐ **PLAN**
☐ **PRACTICE**

Alex A

4mm

· **ORIENTAL PAPERMAKING** ·

There are eight major steps in the hand papermaking process as practiced since 610 CE.

Prints from KAMISUKI CHOHOKI, 1798.

Branches cut and bundled. Outer bark removed. Wood steamed.

Getty-Dubay™ Cursive Italic Lowercase

JOIN 4: *ae* DIAGONAL INTO *e*   Join with a diagonal line into *e*.

ae   ae ce de ee he ie ke le me ne ue ze

Trace and copy.   ae

Mae Lee Julie Katie June Sue
M
Alex Theo Zeke Shelley Renée
A

1. LOOK   ✏ Is your join into **e** a straight diagonal line? *ae*

Joins 1–4 are used here. Dotted lines indicate Joins 5–8.

"Ts'ai Lun conceived the idea of making paper from the bark of trees, discarded cloth and hemp well-prepared." "T

This was written by an ancient Chinese scholar about Ts'ai Lun, a privy councilor to the Royal Court of Ho Ti (89–105 CE).

2. PLAN
3. PRACTICE

OPTION: You may prefer to lift before **e** from the baseline. Avoid a gap, write letters close together.

ae   ae ce de ee ie ke le me ne ue ze · Lee Sue
ae

4mm

White bark separated from core and washed.

Bark beaten and beaten still more into pulp.

Mould dipped in vat of pulp and water.

Getty-Dubay™ Cursive Italic Lowercase

JOIN 5: ōn t̄n f̄n v̄n w̄n x̄n HORIZONTAL
ōu ōo ōa ōz ōt ōl

Join with a horizontal line out of o, t, f, v, w and x into all letters except f.

on

on om or ox · ou oy oi oj op ov ow

Trace and copy. on

oo oa oc od og oq os oz ot ol oh ob ok

oo

Hoa Thor Joy John Lon Solomon

ff

tn

tn tr tu ty ti tw to ta ts tz tl th

The advantage of joining from the crossbar: there is no need to return to cross the t.

tn

tt tt Scott Otto Patty Matthew

Double t

tt

OPTION: You may prefer to join out of the first stroke of t (from the baseline), then add the crossbar after the word is written.

tn (dashed)

tn tn tr tu ty ti tl th to ts te ta

tn

NOTE: In this book t is joined into e in this way.

te · Pete Kate Nate

OPTION: te
OPTION: Lift before e after t. te
See page 27, line 16.
OPTION: Join into two-stroke e. ten
See page 27, line 18.

te

fn

fn fr fu fy fi fj fo fa fs · ft ft or ft ft fl

fn

ff ff ff · Jeff Clifton

OPTION: fe
OPTION: Lift before e after f. fe
See page 27, line 16.
OPTION: Join into two-stroke e. fen
See page 27, line 18.

ff

CHECKLIST
___ shape
___ size
___ slope
___ spacing

4mm

Getty-Dubay™ Cursive Italic Lowercase

vn vn vr · vu vy vi · vo · va vs · vt vl Aviva
Trace and copy. vn

wn wn wr · wu wy wi · wo · wa ws wt wl
wn
wh wk · Lewis Edwin Newton
wn

xn xn · xu xy xi · xo · xa xs · xt xl
xn
Alexis Maxine

1 LOOK ✏ Are you joining with a straight horizontal line? on (AVOID on)

Joins 1-5 are used here. Dotted lines indicate Joins 6-8.

Hand papermaking processes today use plant fibers or rag pulp.

2 PLAN H

3 PRACTICE

NOTE: Join into e out of o, v, w and x with a diagonal join.   OPTION: te fe

oe oe ve we xe · Joe Eve Gwen Axel
oe

OPTION: You may prefer to lift before e after o, t, f, v, w and x.

⌐oe⌐ oe te fe ve we xe · Joe Eve Peter
or Peter (see p.26)
oe

OPTION: You may prefer to use a 2-stroke e after o, t, f, v, w and x.

⌐oe⌐ oe te fe ve we xe · Joe Eve Peter
oe

4mm

Getty-Dubay™ Cursive Italic Lowercase

JOIN 6: rn ru ro ra re **DIAGONAL OUT OF r**
Join with a short diagonal line into all letters except f.

rn | rn rm rr · Arne Carmen Larry
Trace and copy.

ru | ru ry ri rt rv rl rh rb rk · Art

ro ra | ro · ra rc rd rs · Arturo Sara Lars

re | re · Karen Greta

OPTION: If you prefer a 2-stroke e, join into the top of e.

re Karen

re re
waistline
rn (AVOID m rn may look like m or vn)

LOOK at your writing.
Are you joining out of r just below the waistline?
Are you bending the top of r at the waistline?

Joins 1-6 are used here. Dotted lines indicate Joins 7-8.

Hand papermak-
ing mills use this
process today.

NOTE: The join out of r needs more practice than any other join. Legibility depends on it being done well.

· WESTERN PAPERMAKING ·

Deckle frame fits tightly over the mould
Mould Woven brass wires are attached to frame

Vat of pulp water

Cotton or linen rags are beaten in water to form the pulp. The mould and the deckle are immersed in the vat of pulp. A thin layer of pulp is gathered on the mould.

SIDE VIEW — pulp, deckle, mould

The deckle is removed and the mould with the layer of pulp is turned over and rolled onto a piece of felt.

pulp placed on felt

After being pressed, dried, and sized, a piece of paper is ready to write on.

OPTION: You may prefer to lift after r to aid legibility.
Avoid a gap; write letters close together.

ru | ra re ri ro ru ry rr

Larry Sara Karen Greta Arturo Lars

4mm

Getty-Dubay™ Cursive Italic Lowercase

JOIN 7: sn bn pn HORIZONTAL TO DIAGONAL
Join with a horizontal line blending into a diagonal line into all letters except f.

sn
Trace and copy.

sn sm sr or sn sm sr · su sy si st sp sv
sn
sw st sh sb sk · so ss or ss · se · sa sc sd sg
sw
Jessie José Justin J

bn
bn br or bn br · bu by bi bt bl bb · bo bs
bn
be · ba bc bd bg · Pablo Bobby Deborah
be

pn
pn pr or pn pr · pu py pi pt pp pl ph · po
pn
ps or ps · pe · pa pc pd pg · Hope Joseph
ps

LOOK at your writing.

✏ Are you following back out of s, b & p? sr br pr (AVOID br pr)

Joins 1-7 are used here. Dotted lines indicate Join 8.

Wood is the basic raw material from
which most machine made paper is
manufactured. W

Some machine-made papers are made with 100% wood fiber, some 100% cotton rag, and some are mixtures.

OPTION: You may prefer to lift after s, b and p. Avoid a gap; write letters close together.

sa
sa se si so su · ba be bi bo bu · pa pe pi po pu
sa

4mm

Getty-Dubay™ Cursive Italic Lowercase

JOIN 8: aa ac ad ag aq as — DIAGONAL TO HORIZONTAL

Join with a diagonal line blending into the horizontal beginning of **a, c, d, g, q** and **s**.

aa ad | aa ad ca ea ed da dd ha ia id ka

Trace and copy. | aa
la ld ma na nd ua ud za · Shalonda
la

ag aq | ag aq eg eq ig iq ng ug uq · Quang
ag

ac | ac cc ec ic uc · Vic Alice Michael
ac

as | as cs ds es hs is ks ls ms ns us zs
as

Joins 7 & 8 | sa sc ss · ba · pa ps · Lissa Barbara
sa

1. LOOK at your writing. Are your a, c, d, g, q, and s flat on top? ā (AVOID aa or aa)

2. PLAN how to make the joins look more like the models.

All joins are used here.

Our word "pen" is from the Latin word for feather – "penna."

CHECKLIST
___ shape
___ size
___ slope
___ spacing

3. PRACTICE the joins which need more work.

· PENS ·

The first pens were cut from reeds.

Later, flight feathers of geese or swans were used.

Quills were the primary pen used for writing on parchment and paper until the 19th century.

OPTION: You may prefer to lift before **a, c, d, g, q** and **s**. Avoid a gap, write letters close together.

aa | aa ac ad ag aq as · aa

4mm

Getty-Dubay™ Numerals & Number Words

LIFTS: *af az · ga ja qu ya* (NO JOINS)

Lift writing tool before *f* and *z* and after *g, j, q* and *y*.

af — Olaf Jeffrey Alfredo Alfreda
Trace and copy.

az — Alonzo Lizzie Kazuaki Elizabeth
Lift before z from the baseline.

ga ja — Inga Bridget Helge Elijah Sonja

qu ya — Jacqueline Joyce Beryl Lloyd Sylvia

Joins are natural spacers. When letters in a word are not joined, be sure they are close together.   *af az ga ja qu ya*   We read letters from the top (see page 13). For the sake of legibility do not add loops to ascenders.

REVIEW: 8 JOINS Options & Pangram

JOIN 1 — an am ar ax · JOIN 2 OPTIONS: an am ar ax

JOIN 1 — au ay ai at aj ap av aw al ah ak ak ab · JOIN 3 OPTION — ao as

JOIN — ae ae · JOIN 5 — on tn fn vn wn xn · JOIN 6 OPTION — rn rn · JOIN 7 — so bo po

OPTIONS: so bo po · JOIN 8 — aa ac ad ag aq as aa ac ad ag aq as

A quick brown fox jumps over the lazy dog.

Options used here. A quick brown fox jumps over the lazy dog.

4mm

© 2013 Getty-Dubay   31   Getty-Dubay™ Italic Handwriting Series · Book G

Getty-Dubay™ Basic Italic Sentence Practice – Tongue Twisters

GETTY-DUBAY™ CURSIVE ITALIC WRITING PRACTICE

SENATVSPO
IMP·CAESARI·
TRAIANO·AV
MAXIMOTRIB

The Trajan Inscription · Roman Forum
112–113 CE. Cast by Edward Catich (small portion shown)
From THE ROMAN LETTER by James Hayes

The actual height of **S** (top left) is 4 ⅝".

* Note the exception to the horizontal join out of **t**. The join from **t** to one-stroke **e** is from the baseline.

te

Other options:
te te
See pages 26–27.

CHECKLIST
___ shape
___ size
___ slope
___ spacing

The Roman inscriptional letters* serve as the models for our capitals.

They were written with a brush, then incised in the stone and painted.

Square Capitals were derived from the large inscriptional letters.

They were written with a reed pen on parchment and used as a bookhand from the first to the fifth centuries.

SQUARE CAPITALS

4mm

ABCDEFGHIKLMNOPQRSTVXYZ

After Virgil manuscript · 4th century   The 23 letters of the Roman alphabet.

Getty-Dubay™ Cursive Italic

RUSTIC CAPITALS

ABCDEFGHIKLMNOPQRSTUXYZ
After Virgil manuscript 4th-5th century.

Rustics were written with a reed pen on papyrus and parchment.

The flowing, narrow letters of Rustics show the influence of speed and the need to conserve materials. This script was used mainly for special editions of poetry. T

The name Uncial comes from St. Jerome—meaning "inch-high".

We see in Uncial the beginning of our lowercase letters:

a → a, a
d → d
e → e
h → h
m → m
q → q

Uncial writing was used primarily for copies of the Bible. The curving forms show the desire to make letters with the fewest possible strokes. Uncial was used from the third century to the tenth century. U

1. LOOK
2. PLAN
3. PRACTICE

UNCIAL

ABCDEFGHIKLMNOPQRSTUXYZ 4mm
After Gospels of St. Gall—5th-6th century.

Getty-Dubay™ Cursive Italic

abcdefghiklmnopqrſtuxy&z
(long s)

CAROLINGIAN
In the 9th century, an increased interest in culture led to the copying of the Latin classics. This led to the advancement of writing.

The Carolingian script was used for copying large quantities of Latin manuscripts. In use from 800 to 1200, these letters have lengthened ascenders and descenders.

CHECKLIST
____ shape
____ size
____ slope
____ spacing

At its best, Gothic is beautiful but hard to read.

The Gothic script is the bookhand of the late Middle Ages. Its angular letters show the need to save space.

Quite often large letters appear at the beginning of paragraphs.

This Q is from a manuscript written by Claricia, a nun ca. 1200. She represents herself as the tail of the Q. (From WOMEN ARTISTS by K. Peterson and J. Wilson.)

4mm

abcdefghijklmnopqrstuvxyz GOTHIC

Around the 13th century, a faint slash was added to i to aid legibility.

ROTUNDA **abcdefghiklmnopqrstuvxy3**
(round Gothic)

Getty-Dubay™ Italic Handwriting Series · Book G

15TH CENTURY BOOKHAND (HUMANIST BOOKHAND)

abcdefghiklmnopqrſstuxy&z·jvw
(long s)

The scholars collected classical texts— many written in Carolingian. Their Gothic hand (Rotunda) was influenced by the elegant Carolingian to create 15th century bookhand.

A clear, legible bookhand was developed during the Renaissance by Italian scholar-scribes in the fourteenth & fifteenth centuries. It is the basis of many typefaces.

The transition from bookhand to cursive is:
1) round to elliptical forms
O to O
2) vertical to slightly sloped
on to on
3) unjoined to joined.
iu to iu

Italic, a cursive form of this bookhand, flourished for two hundred years as the basic script for business and correspondence. Today it continues as a practical handwriting.

1. LOOK
2. PLAN
3. PRACTICE

ITALIC
Anonymous scribe 1490 (The Houghton Library, Harvard University, Department of Printing and Graphic Arts.) Reproduced by permission.

altior ordo ſacerdotalis · Stephanus qq:
papa ſecundus Romanum imperium
in perſonam magnifici Caroli à Grecis
transtulit in Germanos. Alius iſte Ro·

4mm

Getty-Dubay™ Cursive Italic

[Historical italic script sample:]

Seguita lo essempio delle lre che pono
ligarsi con tutte le sue sequenti, in tal mo=
  do cioe
aa ab ac ad ae af ag ah ai ak al am an
ao ap aq ar as at au ax ay az
Il medesmo farai con d i k l m n u.
Le ligature poi de c f s ſ t sonno
  le infra=
    scritte
et, fa ff fi fm fn fo fr fu fy,
  ſt st
ſſ ſt ß ſt, ta te ti tm tn to tq tr tt tu
  tx ty
Con le restanti littere de lo Alphabeto, che
sono, b e g h o p q r x y z ʒ
non si deue ligar mai lra
  alcuna sequente

ITALIC LA OPERINA, Ludovico degli Arrighi, Italy, 1522
THE FIRST WRITING BOOK by John Howard Benson
(Yale University Press, 1954). Reproduced by permission.

1. The first instruction
2. manual of the italic
3. script was LA OPERINA
4. by Arrighi, printed in
5. Rome in 1522.

Letters above are angular as they were cut and printed from woodblocks.

11. In Italy, italic served as a personal
12. hand for many, including Raphael,
13. Michelangelo and Cellini.

Writing on pages 36–37 offers practice using the baseline only— similar to notebook paper.

NOTE: The two-stroke e is used in this paragraph. (See OPTION page 24.)

18. In England this script became
19. known as the "italique hande." Italic
20. was the hand of courtiers, secretaries
21. and royalty.

CHECKLIST
___ shape
___ size
___ slope
___ spacing

NOTE: After completing page 37, turn to page viii to write the Post-test for your "AFTER" example!

Getty-Dubay™ Italic Handwriting Series · Book G

Getty-Dubay™ Cursive Italic

ROUND HAND
THE UNIVERSAL PENMAN
by George Bickham
(Dover Publications, Inc., New York)
LETTERING: MODES OF WRITING IN WESTERN EUROPE FROM ANTIQUITY TO THE END OF THE 18TH CENTURY by Hermann Degering (Taplinger/Pentalic, 1978). Reproduced by permission.

abcddefoghhijkkllmnnoppqrsfstuvwxyz.
ABCDEFGHIJKLMMM
NNOPQRSTUVWXXYYZ.

During the 17th to 19th centuries, round hand was written with a flexible nib on paper and with an engravers' burin on copperplate.

Round hand was the result of the addition of ornate flourishes, loops on ascenders & descenders, more pen lifts and an extreme slope of 38°.

The looped cursive or "commercial cursive" in use today is patterned after round hand. The loops, extreme slope, and forced joins make looped cursive often illegible when written fast.

"Cursive" comes from the Latin "currere" —to run.

Cursive italic maintains its legibility when written quickly.

Italic handwriting, with its roots in the Renaissance, provides a handsome, graceful script for today. Both basic italic and cursive italic serve well as a practical, legible handwriting.

Italic is a loop free, clean-cut script for the computer age.

NOTE:
To increase writing speed, do Timed Writing exercise on page 38.

You will develop your own unique personal hand. See OPTIONS page 39.

1 LOOK
2 PLAN
3 PRACTICE

Handwriting is a lifelong skill, and good handwriting is a lifelong joy!

✒ Write cursive italic with an edged pen.
4mm

See EDGED PEN ITALIC pages 42-55.

TIMED WRITING
Use the timed writing to help increase speed for formal, informal & rapid writing.

Begin by writing the following sentence on another sheet of paper as a warm-up for the timed writing. If you prefer, substitute another pangram or sentence.

A quick brown fox jumps over the lazy dog.

1. TIME LENGTH: 1 MINUTE Write the sentence at your most comfortable speed. If you finish before the time is up, begin the sentence again.

___

Count the number of words written and write the number in Box 1. **Box 1**

2. TIME LENGTH: 1 MINUTE Write the sentence a little faster. Try to add 1 or 2 more words to your total.

___

Write the number of words written in Box 2. **Box 2**

3. TIME LENGTH: 1 MINUTE Write the sentence as fast as you can. Maintain legibility.

___

Write the number of words written in Box 3. **Box 3**

4. TIME LENGTH: 1 MINUTE Write the sentence at a comfortable speed.

___

Write number of words written in Box 4. **Box 4**

The goal is to increase the number of words written per minute. Aim for an increase in the total of Box 4 over Box 1. Speed can be increased while maintaining legibility. Repeat process often.

EYES CLOSED Using the same sentence, do this exercise as a follow-up to timed writing. Begin with a non-lined sheet of paper. Close your eyes. Picture in your mind's eye the shape of each letter as you write. Take all the time you need. You may be amazed how well you can write with your eyes closed.

GETTY-DUBAY™ ITALIC HANDWRITING OPTIONS
A personal handwriting style is created by variations of shape, size, slope, spacing and speed.

SHAPE
Italic is based on an elliptical shape which may be standard, expanded, or compressed.

Standard — a quick brown fox jumps over the lazy dog

Expanded — a quick brown fox jumps over the

Compressed — a quick brown fox jumps over the lazy dog

SIZE
Each person has a comfortable letter size.

4mm 3mm 2½mm

a quick brown fox jumps over the lazy dog

SLOPE
Writing slope may vary from 0° to 15°. Standard slope is 5°. Whichever slope is preferred, be consistent. See *Slope Guidelines*, page 40.

0° — a quick brown fox jumps over the lazy dog

5° (standard) — a quick brown fox jumps over the lazy dog

10° — a quick brown fox jumps over the lazy dog

15° — a quick brown fox jumps over the lazy dog

SPACING
The spacing between letters in a word and between words may be standard, expanded, or compressed. See *Spacing Guidelines*, page 40.

Standard spacing — a quick brown fox jumps over the lazy dog

Expanded spacing — a quick brown fox jumps over the

Compressed spacing — a quick brown fox jumps over the lazy dog

SPEED
Let the speed of writing fit the need, maintaining legibility. Notice how speed affects shape, size, slope, and spacing.

Moderate speed — a quick brown fox jumps over the lazy dog

Rapid speed — a quick brown fox jumps over the lazy

As you progress, italic handwriting becomes personal and unique. Whichever combinations of options are used, the goal is even shape, even size, even slope and even spacing.

GETTY-DUBAY™ SLOPE GUIDELINES

The *Getty-Dubay™ italic Handwriting Series* is written with a 5° slope. Both basic italic and cursive italic are written with the same 5° slope—there is no need to change.

OPTIONS: The *Getty Dubay italic Handwriting Series* offers a choice of slope—from a vertical of 0° to a slope of 15°. *Slope Guidelines* are shown on page 60. Whichever slope is preferred, the goal is to maintain

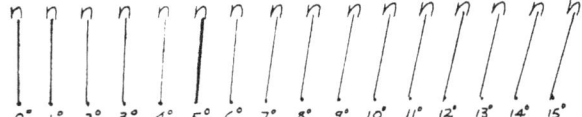

NOTE: As we write we all vary slightly from our chosen slope. We are not machines! An overall, even, balanced writing is our goal. See OPTIONS, page 39.

ASSESSMENT: LOOK at your writing. Are you writing with an even slope? Are you using a 5° slope? What is your choice of slope?
If the slope is uneven, use the following exercise to find your natural slope:
1. Write a word.
2. Check the consistency of the slope by drawing slope lines through the center of each letter (line up with the downstroke or axis of each letter).

3. Choose the slope which appears most often, as in Example A or choose the slope in the middle range, as in Example B.
4. Then draw parallel lines next to the slope you have chosen.
5. Use the parallel lines as your slope guide.

	EXAMPLE A	EXAMPLE B
1. Write word.	slope	slope
2. Draw slope lines over letters	slope	slope
3. Pick one slope	slope	slope
4. Draw parallel lines	|||||	|||||
5. Write over slope lines	slope	slope

PLAN how to write with an even slope.
Use a slope guide under the writing paper. If the slope is more than 15° or a backhand is used, changing the paper position often helps. (Generally, a backhand slope is difficult to read; a slight backhand slope is acceptable.)

As you progress, the goal is to write with a consistent slope of your choice (between 0° and 15°).

GETTY-DUBAY™ SPACING GUIDELINES

There are two aspects of spacing: the space between letters within a word and the space between words in a sentence.

Space between letters:
The letters within a word are close together. In basic italic, there are three rules of spacing:

1. Two downstrokes are the farthest apart.
2. A downstroke and a curve are a little closer.
3. Two curves are the closest, almost touching.

Spaces 1, 2, & 3 equal in area

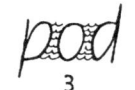

In cursive italic, joins are natural spacers. When lifts occur between letters (before **f** and **z**; after **g, j, q** and **y**), keep letters close together to avoid gaps.

Space between words:
Leave the width of **n** between words.

Use the width of an n between words.

OPTIONS: Standard spacing is used in this book. Expanded and compressed spacing are other choices.

standard   standard
expanded expand
compressed compressed

In the space below write with your most comfortable spacing. Aim for even, balanced writing.

· abcdefghijklmnopqrstuvwxyz ·

PART THREE

Getty-Dubay™
Edged Pen Italic

Italic with the Edged Pen
Basic Italic
Cursive Italic
Chancery Cursive
Pangrams
Personal Correspondence
Greeting Card and Booklet

· abcdefghijklmnopqrstuvwxyz ·

GETTY-DUBAY™ ITALIC HANDWRITING WITH THE EDGED PEN
writing tools / inks / papers / how to sit / pen hold & pen angle

WRITING WITH AN EDGED PEN will help make your handwriting look handsome, beautiful, official! You'll need to spend time developing the correct pen hold and using the letters — but you'll probably find it will be well worth the cost of pen, ink & paper. You can bring yourself and others pleasure through your writing.

WRITING TOOLS

Many edged tools are available — fiber and felt-tip pens, cartridge ink pens, fountain pens and dip nibs. (A nib is a pen tip.) You can also cut your own pens from ice cream sticks, tongue depressors, paint stir sticks, cattail stalks, green garden stakes, bamboo reeds, etc. A few are shown below:

The left-handed person may find left oblique nibs helpful, but the square cut nibs can be used.

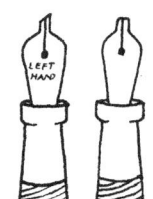 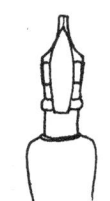 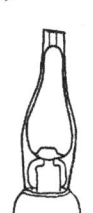 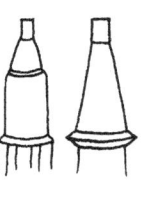 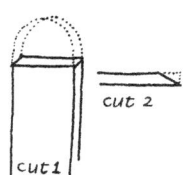  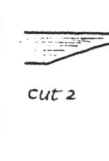

FOUNTAIN PENS   PENHOLDERS WITH DIP NIBS   FIBER-TIP PENS   TONGUE DEPRESSOR   CATTAIL STALK (for large letters)

INKS

Be sure to use fountain pen ink in fountain pens. If you're using a dip nib, use ink that is *not* waterproof (unless you need your writing waterproofed). Waterproof inks generally contain shellac and tend to clog dip pens — and ruin fountain pens. You can learn to write with any kind of ink. Be sure to stir the bottle before using and replace the cap after each use. Black and many colors are available. Try mixing two colors of the same type and brand to create your own color.

PAPERS

For practice, white typing paper or a bond paper will usually provide a suitable writing surface. Avoid onionskin and easy-to-erase paper. The best way to select paper is to write on a sample piece to see if it takes ink well and does not feather. Colored papers can add interest to your writing — try colored butcher paper for large signs. Construction paper is usually too rough and porous. Most papers are machine made, but a few are made by hand. *See pp. 36, 37 and 40 for more information about papermaking.*

Both letters 1 & 2 were written with the same pen on different paper. → ¹ n ² n *feathering*

HOW TO SIT

Rest your forearms on the writing surface, feet flat on the floor and keep your back comfortably straight as you lean slightly forward.

It is easier to get the entire edge of your pen nib on the surface of your paper if you write on a slanted board.

If you are left-handed, try either paper position A, B, or somewhere in between. If you write from above the line, hold paper similar to C or D.

 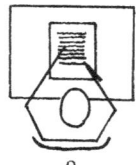

If you are right-handed, use paper position C for rapid everyday writing. For careful (formal) work, hold paper as in D.

PENHOLD & ANGLE

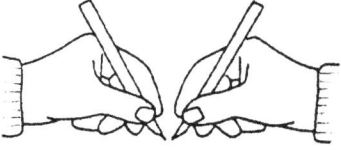

Hold your pen with thumb and index finger resting it on the middle finger. Rest the shaft near the large knuckle.

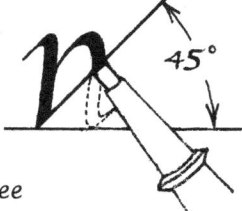

Pen edge lies at 45° angle to the writing line. This allows pen edge to form the correct thicks and thins as you write lowercase letters.

Upon completion of this book, for further study in edged pen writing see
Getty-Dubay Italic Calligraphy: for School & Home and
Italic Letters: Calligraphy & Handwriting.

GETTY-DUBAY™ BASIC ITALIC – EDGED PEN

GUIDELINES

The body height of italic lowercase letters is generally four or five pen widths regardless of the size of the pen. The pen is held horizontally to mark off the pen widths to measure the distance between guidelines.

Guidelines:

BASIC ITALIC — aghf P

CURSIVE ITALIC — aghf P

In this book the ascender and descender lines are not shown since ascenders and descenders have been shortened. The shortened letters allow you to write faster. If you are carefully writing out a poem, quotation, etc., you may wish to extend your ascenders and descenders to 4 or 5 pen widths each.

Caps are always written 1½ times body height of lowercase.

Calligraphy – beautiful writing.
extended ascenders and descenders

BASIC STROKES

Don't shift pen or arm – keep pen edge at a constant 45° pen edge angle to the baseline.

Trace & copy.

BASIC ITALIC

See pages 2-5 for lowercase families.

i i   j j   l l · k k or k k   v v   w w   x x   z z

To write the size shown on lines 1-13, use a fine nib. Dip nibs are also available in this size.

h h   m m   n n   r r · u u   y y · b b   p p

a a   d d   g g   q q · e or e   o o   c c   s s · f f   t t

See page 6 for capital families.

C D G O Q · M W · A H K N T U V X Y Z

overlap at A & B

Flatten pen edge angle between 15°-30° for caps.* (But stay at 45° for rapid writing.)

E F L B P R R S J · 0 1 2 3 4 5 6 7 8 9 9 · . , ? ! " "

Alphabet Sentence

A quick brown fox jumps over the lazy dog.
or k

* To flatten pen edge angle to 15°-30°, keep the *same* pen hold, but:
LEFT-HANDED · move elbow away from your body to flatten pen edge angle.
RIGHT-HANDED · move right elbow closer to your body.

This page intentionally left blank.

GETTY-DUBAY™ CURSIVE ITALIC - EDGED PEN

BASIC STROKES
Trace & copy each line of writing.

SERIF ALPHABET

a b c d e f g h i j k l m n o p q r s t u v w x y z

ENTRANCE SERIFS
Roll into m, n, r, x.

mmm   nnnn   rrrr   xxxx or x

EXIT SERIFS
Roll out of a, d, h, i, k, l, m, n, u, z.

aaaa   ddd   hhh   iii   kk or k

lll   mm   nnn   uuu   zzz

SHARP ENTRANCE SERIFS
Angle up into j, p, v, w.

jjjj   ppp   vvvv   wwww

NO CHANGE
These letters remain the same as the basic italic letterforms, except the f now descends below the baseline.

bbb   ccc   eee or eee   ggg   ooo

qqq   sss   tt   yyy   fff

JOINS

Lowercase letters are joined together for cursive handwriting.

JOIN 1
Diagonal - roll over into m, n, r and x.

an · am an ar ax or ax

JOIN 2
Diagonal - swing up into b, h, i, j, k, l, p, t, u, v, w and y.

au · ab ah ai aj ak al ap at au av

aw ay · OPTION: an am ar ax

4mm

This page intentionally left blank.

Getty-Dubay™ Cursive Italic – Edged Pen

JOIN 3
Diagonal - start back into o and s.

ao · ao as · OPTION: ae

JOIN 4
Diagonal into e.

ae · ae ee ie ue te

JOIN 5
Horizontal out of f, o, t, v, w and x.

fn · fn on tn vn wn xn

JOIN 6
Diagonal out of r.

rn · ra re ri ro ru rz

JOIN 7
Horizontal to diagonal out of b, p and s.

sn · bn pn sn

JOIN 8
Diagonal into horizontal top of a, c, d, g, q and s.

aa · aa ac ad ag aq as

LIFTS
Lift before f and z. Lift after g, j, q and y.

af az · gn jn qu yn

EXERCISE

For more practice with joins, see pages 21-31. Use lines on page 55 or 56 as a lined sheet under your writing paper.

ana bnb cnc dnd ene fnf gng hnh ini

jnj knk lnl mnm nnn ono pnp qnq rnr

sns tnt unu vnv wnw xnx yny & znz

SENTENCE PRACTICE

Thomas Carlyle 1795-1881 Scottish essayist & historian.

Certainly the art of writing is the most miraculous of all things man has devised.

~: Examples for training the Hand :~

A·aabcdee·fg hiklmnopqpg

orstuxxyz & st sl ss tu w

No Glory comes at the start, but at the end.
Thus is born honor, true &
perfect:
Why enter the field of battle, & then flee?

Ille Idem L Vicetinus Scribebat Rome.

Translation by John Howard Benson of LA OPERINA by Ludovico degli Arrighi, Rome, 1522. THE FIRST WRITING BOOK by John Howard Benson (Yale University Press, 1955.) Reproduced by permission.

Writing with an edged pen at a 45° angle creates a thin line for the diagonal join — a pleasing contrast.

an

For a thinner horizontal line, flatten the pen edge angle slightly for the crossbar of f and t and also for Join 5 (similar to pen edge angle for capitals, page 43).

4mm

This page intentionally left blank.

Getty-Dubay™ Cursive Italic – Edged Pen

CURSIVE CAPITALS

A B C D E F G H I or I J or J K
L M N O P Q R R S T U or U V
W X Y or Y or Y Z

Use these caps with lowercase only.
Don't write entire words with these caps.

Flatten pen edge angle between 15° and 30° for carefully written caps. Stay at 45° for rapid writing.

Lowercase joins: abcdefghijklmnopqrstuvwxyz

CAPITAL PRACTICE

Amazon Brazos Columbia Danube

Principal rivers of the world written with a "fine" nib.

Euphrates Fraser Ganges Huang Ho

OPTION: You may prefer a 2-stroke e with the edged pen,

ae ae

with a flourish out of e.

Indus Juruá Kolyma Loire or Loire two-stroke e

Mississippi Nile Orinoco Paraná

Quarai Rhine Snake Tigrus Ural

OPTION: You may prefer to begin i, u, and y with a serif.

i, u, y

Volga White Xingu Yukon Zambezi

4mm

SENTENCE PRACTICE

A true source of human happiness lies in taking a genuine interest in all the details of daily life and elevating them by art. WILLIAM MORRIS

Written with an "extra fine" nib.

3mm

This page intentionally left blank.

CHANCERY CURSIVE

In the 15th and 16th centuries, the chancery cursive hand developed. The chancery was the office where official documents were kept, and chancery cursive was the official handwriting for these records.

FLOURISHED ASCENDERS & DESCENDERS

A flourish is a flowing curve.   *Add beginning serifs on i, u and y.*

bb dd hh kk ll ff gg jj pp ii uu yy

ASCENDERS: With a dip pen, move slightly to the right before moving left.

CHANCERY LOWERCASE

abcdefghijklmnopqrstuvwxyz

NOTE: Ascenders are taller and descenders are longer.

CHANCERY CAPITALS

AA BB CC DD EE FF GG

Trace & write:

For carefully written caps, flatten pen edge angle to 15°-30°. Stay at 45° for rapid writing.

GG HH II or JJ or JJ KK LL

Be sure this is a sharp angle on H, K, M, N, U, V, W.

MM N OO PP QQ QQ RR

Keep horizontals straight except for slight curve at A & B.

SS TT UU VV WW XX YY Z

There are many different choices of Chancery caps.

SENTENCE PRACTICE

Arrighi's La Operina, the first italic instruction manual, was published in Rome in 1522.

The first italic instruction book was written by Ludovico degli Arrighi (Vincentino). It is printed from wood blocks, therefore, it is thought the letters appear more angular than the actual handwriting of that time.

4mm

Remember, your handwriting is a personal statement. For careful (formal) writing, you may choose to use fewer joins.

From LA OPERINA by Ludovico degli Arrighi, Rome, 1522. THE FIRST WRITING BOOK by John Howard Benson (Yale University Press, 1955.) Reproduced by permission.

This page intentionally left blank.

PANGRAMS
Each sentence contains all 26 letters of the alphabet.

BASIC ITALIC

NOTE:
2-stroke k on line 1; 1-stroke k on line 3.

Quick wafting zephyrs vex bold Jim.

Picking just six quinces, new farmhand proves strong but lazy.

1. LOOK at your writing.
2. PLAN which letters need work.
3. PRACTICE those letters on lined paper.

A large fawn jumped quickly over white zinc boxes.

CURSIVE ITALIC

NOTE:
2-stroke e in "very."

Fred specialized in the job of making very quaint wax trays.

NOTE:
Lift after w in "vowed."

Six crazy kings vowed to abolish my quite pitiful jousts.

Jack amazed a few girls and boys by dropping the antique onyx vase.

This page intentionally left blank.

Getty-Dubay™ Cursive Italic – Edged Pen Pangrams

Many big jackdaws quickly zipped over the fox pen.

Five or six big jet planes zoomed quickly by the new tower.

CHECKLIST
____ shape
____ size
____ slope
____ spacing

CHANCERY CURSIVE

Waltz, nymph, for quick jigs vex Bud.

Frowzy things plumb vex'd Jack Q.

I quickly explained that many big jobs involve few hazards.

NOTE: 2-stroke e in "vex'd."

Shortest panagram! Count the number of letters!

UNJOINED CHANCERY

A quick brown fox jumps over the lazy dog.

Quickly pack the box with five dozen modern jugs.

For further practice, use

Italic Letters: Calligraphy & Handwriting

or

Getty-Dubay™ Italic Calligraphy: for School & Home.

4mm

* www.handwritingsuccess.com

PERSONAL CORRESPONDENCE

One of the anticipations of each weekday is checking the mail. How grand it is when we receive a handwritten message from a friend. You can bring joy into the lives of others with a cheery note or letter — and you can practice your handwriting at the same time. Surprise a friend with your words!

WRITE LETTERS ON LONG STRIPS

Use them for letters. Write on! • Dear Reader, Not all letters have to be written on standard sizes sheets of paper. Sometimes print shops will sell or give you endcuts.

Sometimes messages can be written at random. Not all of your correspondence has to be designed the same.

Dan

Put a surprise in the envelope by designing your own format.

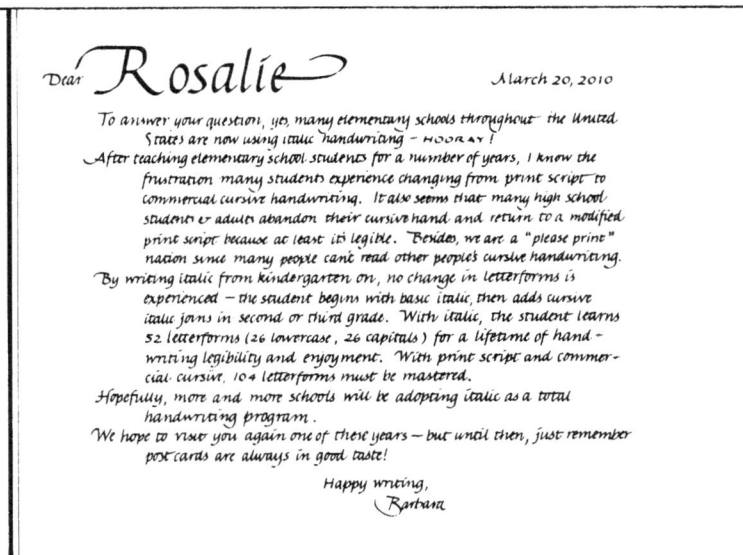

There's more to it than just wiggling your fingers and out come the letters — HOWARD GLASSER

Dear Dan, I understand you're learning italic handwriting. TERRIFIC! One of the best ways to exercise your new skill is by writing notes and letters to your friends. You might write a short quote on the left with a wider pen, then the text at the right as I have written here. Love, Barbara 15·IX·10

quoted with permission of Howard Glasser

See Pop-up card designs INSTRUCTION MANUAL, page 85.

ENVELOPES

Design your own envelope by using a commercial envelope for a pattern. Cut your envelopes from plain paper, gift wrap paper, or large magazine covers. For the last two papers, use a self-sticking label for the address & attach the stamp with adhesive.

Note: The state and zip code should be written on the same line.

GREETING CARD

To make a greeting card for a business size envelope, 10.5 cm x 24 cm (4 1/8 x 8 1/2 in), you will need:
- scissors
- yarn or thread, 90 cm (35 1/2 in)
- needle
- ruler
- paper clips
- 1 sheet typing paper (or similar) cut to 19 cm x 22 cm (7 1/2 in x 8 3/4 in) for inside of card
- 1 sheet colored paper (heavier than typing) cut to 20 cm x 23 cm (8 x 9 in) for cover of card

a. Fold both sheets lengthwise and crease.
b. Insert typing paper inside cover.
c. Paper clip sheets together.
d. On the inside, make a center dot A and one on either side at equal distances from the center, BC.
e. Push needle through the 3 dots ABC to establish stitching holes.
f. Stitch sheets together as follows:
   1) From outside cover, pass needle through center hole A, leaving 15 cm (6 in) for tying.
   2) From inside, pass needle through hole B to outside of card.
   3) From outside, skip over A, pass needle through third hole C to inside.
   4) From inside, pass needle through center hole A to outside.
   5) Tie knot over the long stitch. Tie in bow as shown.
g. Complete cover and inside message before or after stitching.

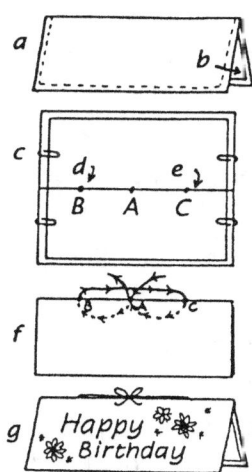

SMALL BOOK

Add a few more inside pages as in illustration b. You may fold all of your sheets either direction:

 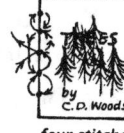

two stitches   four stitches

The four-stitch bookbinding is a bit stronger—tighten each stitch as you go along. Decorate your cover with a drawing, potato print, etc.

SURPRISE BOOKLET

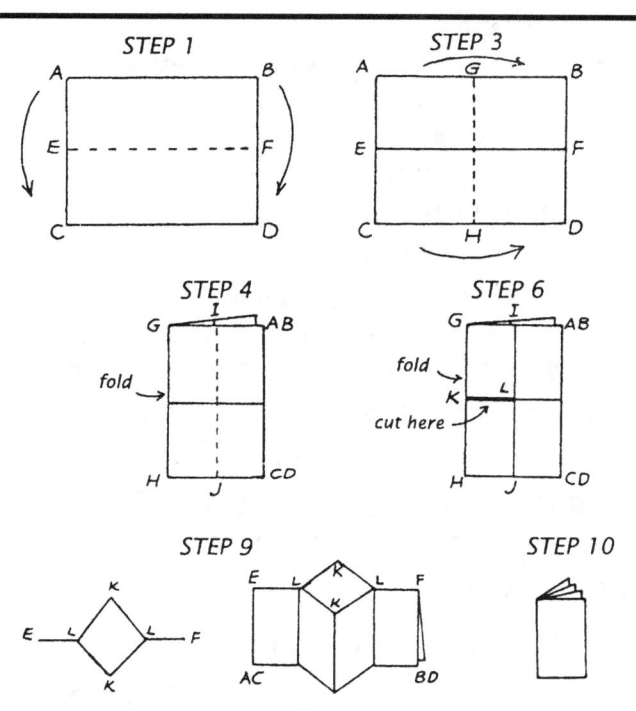

top view   front view   completed booklet

NOTE: In illustrations above, dotted line indicates fold that occurs within the given step. Solid lines within rectangle indicate folds previously established.

See INSTRUCTION MANUAL: Envelope Instructions, p. 81, and Envelope Pattern (A2 size) p. 108.

Use as a small booklet, greeting card, or personal note.
Materials: sheet of light or medium weight paper and scissors.
A 28 cm x 43 cm (11" x 17") sheet will give a finished size of 10.8 cm x 14 cm (4 1/4" x 5 1/2"). This size will fit an A-2 envelope.

1. Fold AB to CD to establish EF.
2. Open back to original size.
3. Fold AC to BD to establish GH.
4. Fold GH to AC/BD to establish IJ.
5. Open to previous fold (GH/AB/CD).
6. With scissors, cut KL by cutting halfway between GH, stopping at fold IJ.
7. Open to original size ABCD.
8. Refold AB to CD as in #1.
9. Grasp E/AC with left hand and F/BD with right hand, then push hands together, establishing three leaves on one side and one on the other.
10. Fold remaining leaf over the other three pages. Two leaves have folds at the top and two on the fore edge of the booklet.

beginning of letter   middle of letter   end of letter

GLOSSARY

ASCENDER • The part of a letter that extends above the waistline.

ARCH • The part of a letter resembling an arch, such as the round portion of "n."

BASELINE • The line on which letters "sit," bottom line of body height (sometimes called the writing line).

BASIC ITALIC • A form of unjoined writing using italic letters without entrance or exit serifs.

BODY HEIGHT • The distance between baseline and waistline (sometimes called "x" height).

BRANCHING LINE • An imaginary line halfway between the baseline and waistline.

CALLIGRAPHY • Beautiful or elegant writing, also the art of producing such writing. The letters are generally unjoined and often written with the edged tool. Italic calligraphy is one type of formal hand lettering or writing.

CAPITAL LETTER • A letter in the series **A,B,C**, rather than **a,b,c** (sometimes called upper-case, large letters, or caps).

COUNTER • Partially or fully enclosed space within a letter.

CROSSBAR • A horizontal line, second stroke of **f** and **t**.

CURSIVE ITALIC • A form of joined writing using italic letters with entrance and exit serifs. [Medieval Latin SCRIPTA CURSIVA - "Flowing script" - from Latin CURSUS, past participle of CURRERE - "to run."] Four characteristics of a cursive hand are elliptical forms, slight slope, fluent (mostly one-stroke letters), and joined letters.

DESCENDER • The part of a letter that extends below the baseline.

DIAGONAL • A line from lower left to upper right (as used in joins and letter shapes) or a line from upper left to lower right (as used in letter shapes).

DOWNSTROKE • A line from top to bottom following letter slope angle.

ELLIPTICAL SHAPE • A line following a compressed circular shape or elongated circle (as in *o*).

HORIZONTAL • A line extending from left to right, parallel to baseline and waistline.

INTERSPACE • An area between letters within words.

INVERTED ARCH • The part of a letter resembling an upside-down arch such as "u."

ITALIC • A script originating in Italy in the late 15th and early 16th centuries. It is characterized by slightly sloped, elliptical, fluent and often joined letterforms.

ITALIC HANDWRITING • A system of writing for everyday use incorporating both an unjoined form of writing (basic italic) and a cursive form of writing (cursive italic).

JOT • A short diagonal above i and j in place of a dot.

LETTER DIMENSIONS
   SHAPE • The correct form of a capital or lower-case letter.
   SIZE • The height and width of a letter.
   SLOPE • The slant of a letter.
   SPACING • The space between letters in words and space between words in a sentence.
   SPEED • The rate of writing.

LOWERCASE LETTER • A letter in the series **a, b, c**, rather than **A, B, C** (sometimes called small letters). [From the printer's practice of keeping the small letters in lower type cases or drawers.]

PEN EDGE ANGLE • The angle of the edge of the pen nib in relation to the baseline.

SANS SERIF • Without serifs, without any additions to the letter, as in basic italic.

SERIF • An entrance or exit stroke of a letter.

STROKE • Any straight or curved written line.

UPPERCASE • See CAPITAL LETTER. [From the printer's practice of keeping the large letters in the upper type cases or drawers.]

WAISTLINE • The top line of the body height.

Anderson, Donald M. *Calligraphy: The Art of Written Forms.* New York: Dover Publications, 1992.

Anderson, Donna. "The Italic's Answer to Illegibility." *Vancouver Sun* (B.C.), February 21, 1976.

Benson, John Howard. *The First Writing Book, An English Translation & Fascimile Text of Arrighi's Operina, The First Manual of the Chancery Hand.* New Haven: Yale University Press, 1955.

Catich, Edward M., *The Origin of the Serif.* Davenport, Iowa: The Catfish Press, St. Ambrose College, 1993. Originally published 1968.

Dubay, Inga and Barbara Getty. *Italic Letters: Calligraphy and Handwriting.* Portland, Oregon: Continuing Education Press, Portland State University, 1992.

Dubay, Inga. "The Write Stuff." Op-Ed. *The New York Times.* September 8, 2009.

Edwards, Betty. *Drawing On the Right Side of the Brain.* Los Angeles: J.P.Tarcher, Inc., 1979.

Encyclopaedia Britannica s.v. "Numerals." Chigago: Encyclopaedia Britannica, Inc., 1993. 8: 826–27.

Fairbank, Alfred. *A Handwriting Manual.* New York: Watson-Guptill Publications, 1975.

Getty, Barbara. "A Case for Legibility." *Oregon Elementary Principal.* (Fall, 1979): 19-20.

Florey, Kitty Burns, *Script & Scribble: The Rise and Fall of Handwriting.* Brooklyn: Melville House Publishing, 2009, 2013.

Getty, Barbara and Inga Dubay. *Getty-Dubay™ Italic Handwriting Series (Books A, B, C, D, E, F, G and INSTRUCTION MANUAL).* 4th ed. Portland, Oregon. Getty-Dubay™ Productions, 2009-2013.

———. *Italic Handwriting Series (Books A, B, C, D, E, F, G and INSTRUCTION MANUAL).* 3rd ed. Portland, Oregon. Continuing Education Press, Portland State University, 1994.

———. *Write Now: The Complete Program for Better Handwriting.* Portland, Oregon. Continuing Education Press, Portland State University. 1991, Rev. Ed., 2005.

———. *Write Now: The Getty-Dubay™ Program for Handwriting Success.* Portland, Oregon. Getty-Dubay™ Productions. 2011.

Groff, Patrick J. "Preference for Handwriting Styles by Big Business." *Elementary English,* 41 (December, 1964): 863-64, 868.

Hayes, James. *The Roman Letter.* Chicago: The Lakeside Press. n.d.

Jarman, Christopher J. *The Development of Handwriting Skills,* Great Britain: Basil Blackwell,1979.

———. *Fun with Pens.* New York: Taplinger Publishing Co., 1979.

Lehman, Charles L., with contributing authors Donald Cowles and Gertrude Hildreth. *Handwriting Models for Schools.* Portland, Oregon: The Alcuin Press, 1976.

Petersen, Karen & J. J. Wilson. *Women Artists: Recognition and Reappraisal from the Early Middle Ages to the Twentieth Century.* New York: New York University Press/Harper & Row, 1976.

Reynolds, Lloyd J. *Italic Calligraphy and Handwriting.* New York: Pentalic, 1969.

Temple, Charles A., Ruth G. Nathan, and Nancy A. Burris. *The Beginnings of Writing.* Boston: Allyn and Bacon, Inc., 1982.

Ullman, B.L. *Ancient Writing and its Influence.* New York: Cooper Square Publishers, Inc. 1963.

Wallace, Don. "Sending The Right Message," *Success Magazine,* 62 (April 1989).

Getty-Dubay™ Italic Handwriting

5° Letter Slope Lines

Getty-Dubay™ Italic Handwriting
5mm lines

Getty-Dubay™ Italic Handwriting
4mm lines

www.ingramcontent.com/pod-product-compliance
Lightning Source LLC
Chambersburg PA
CBHW051422070526
44584CB00023B/3546